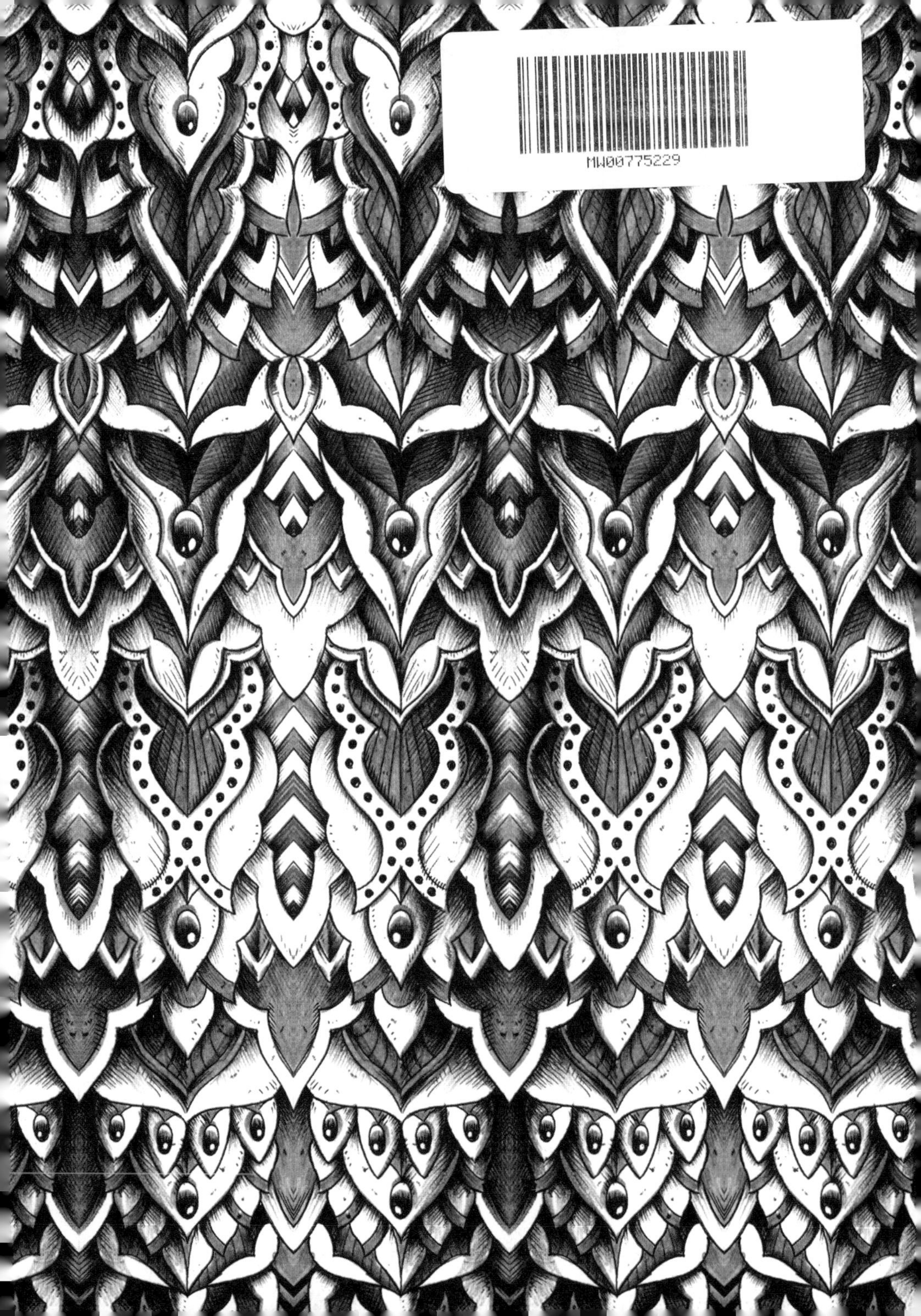

The remembrances
and thoughts of:

*A J lah*

"Fill your paper with the breathings
of your heart."

**—William Wordsworth**

FEATURING THE DESIGNS OF BEN KWOK

elifonts have very long nosies. they have very big ears. elifonts are gray. elifonts have horns riet next thir naise. elifonts live in Affica. elifonts are about 10 feet tall.

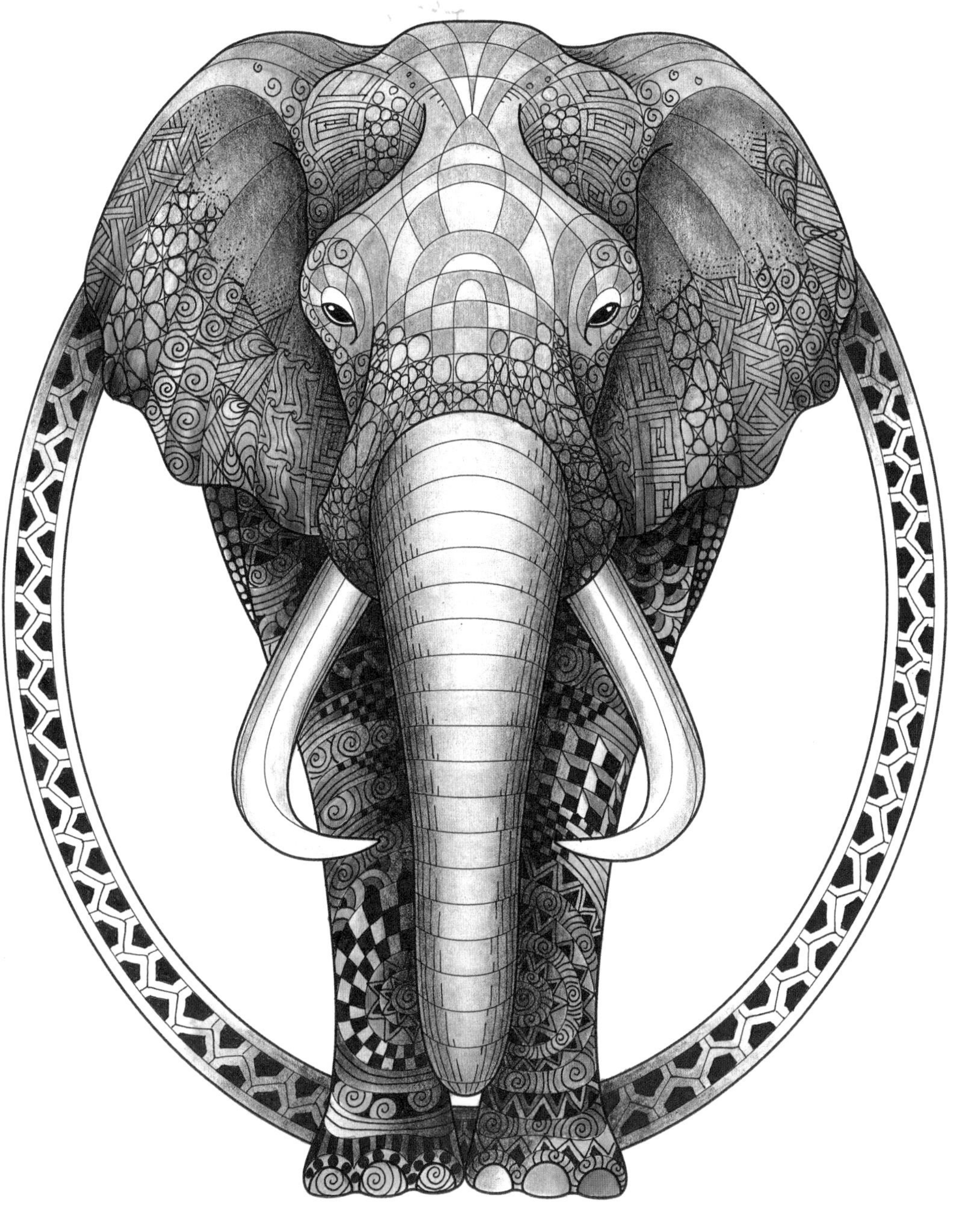

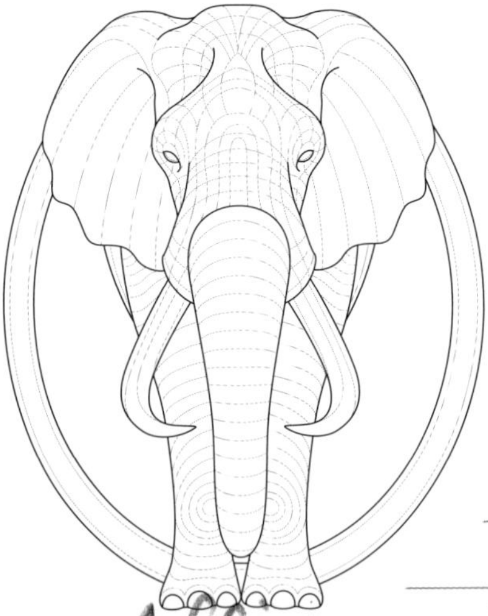

Afica

in Africa
A Lot
of animals
live thir
like elifants.
Lions also
Live in
Africa. Thar are
so many animals
I could right
Down one more
hippes Live in
Africa too. so
many Animals right.
I Love Animals so
so much Do yea?.

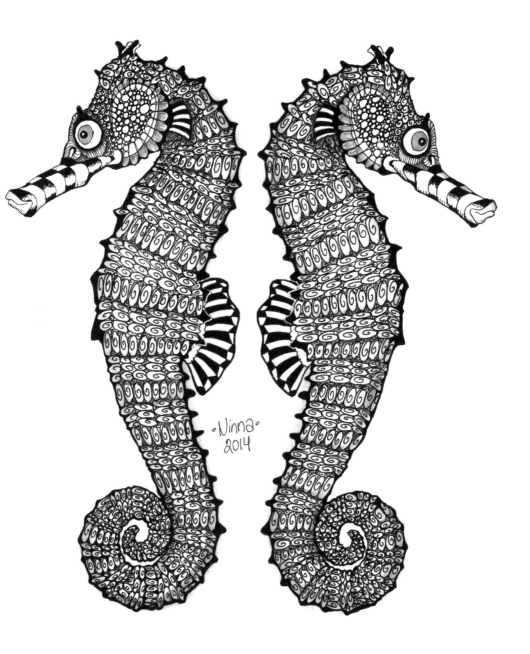

Ninna
2014

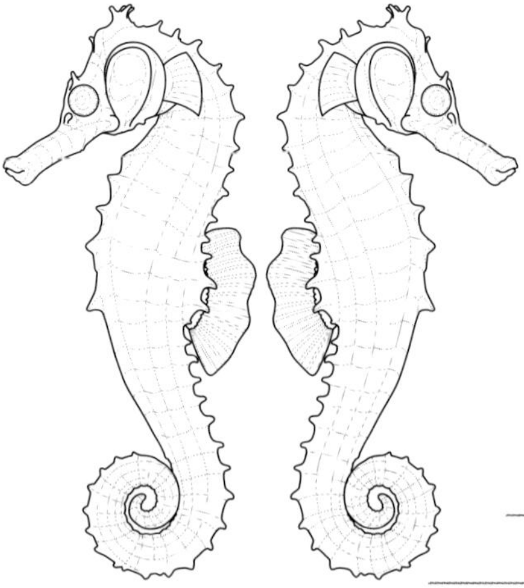

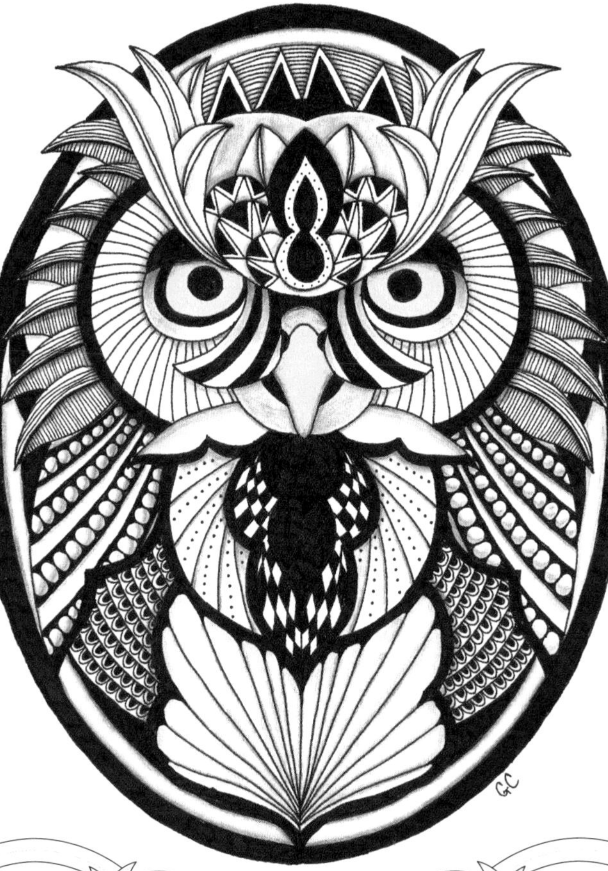
GC
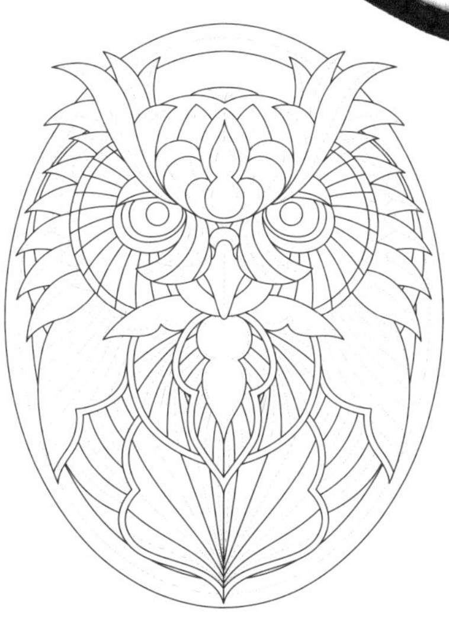
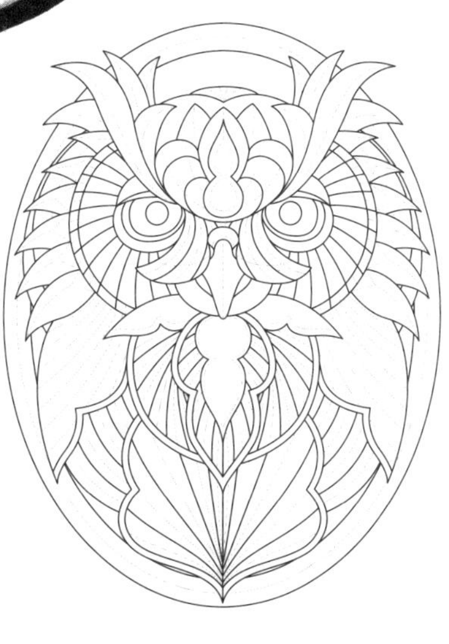

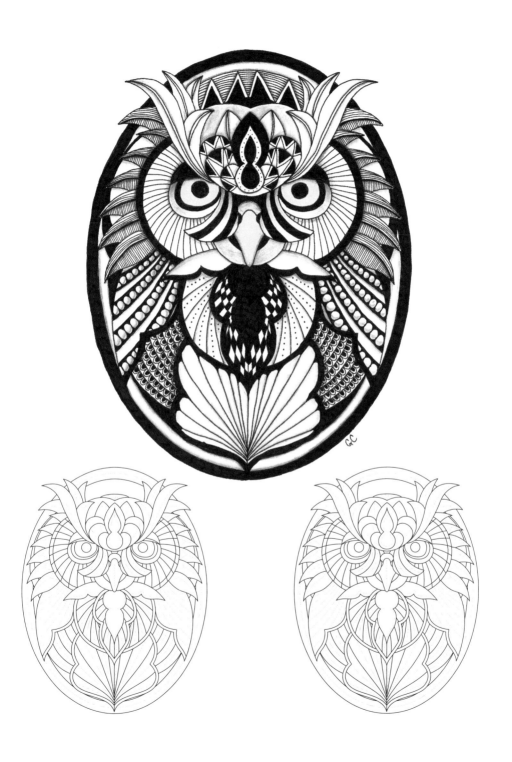

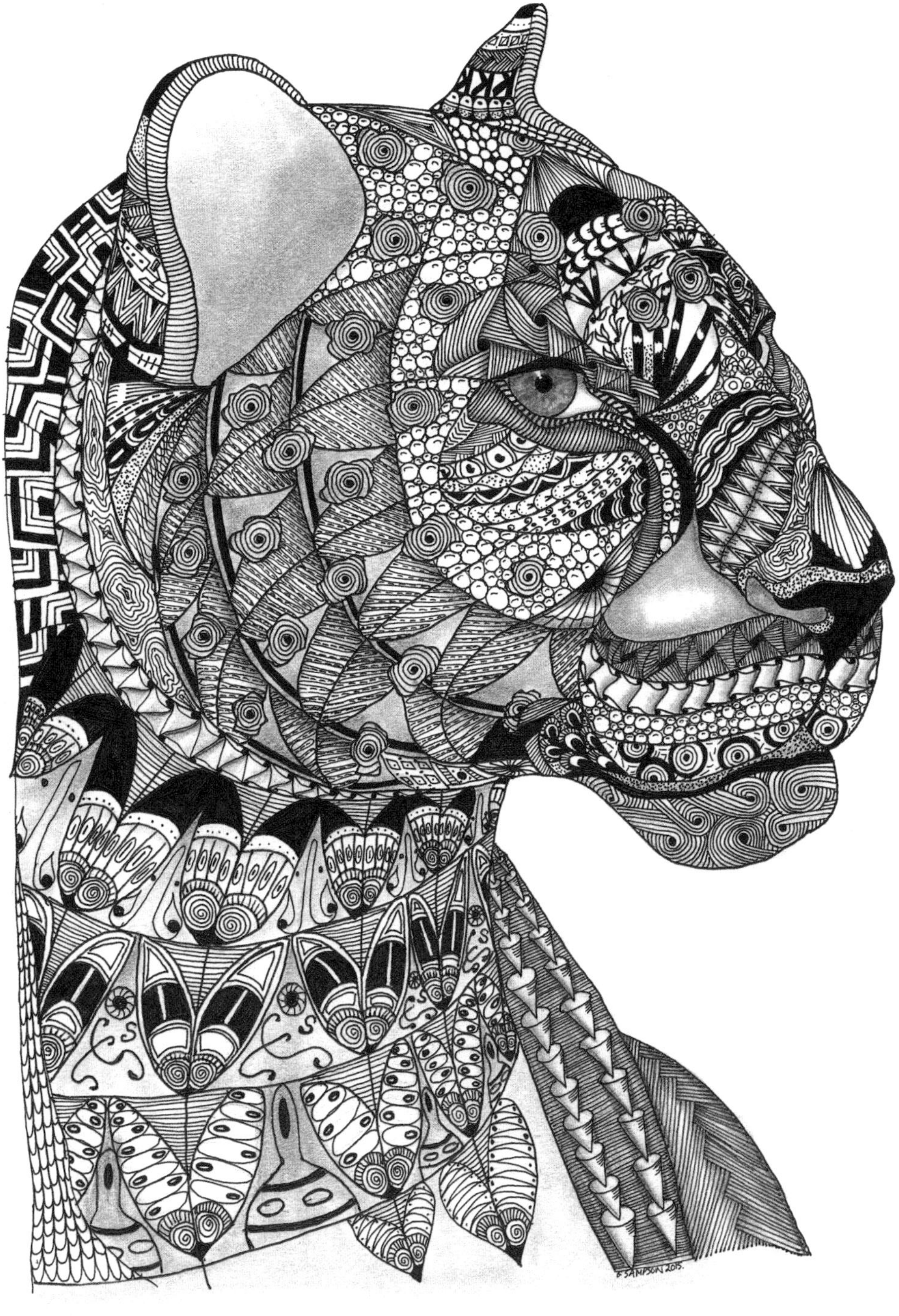
B SAMPSON 2015.

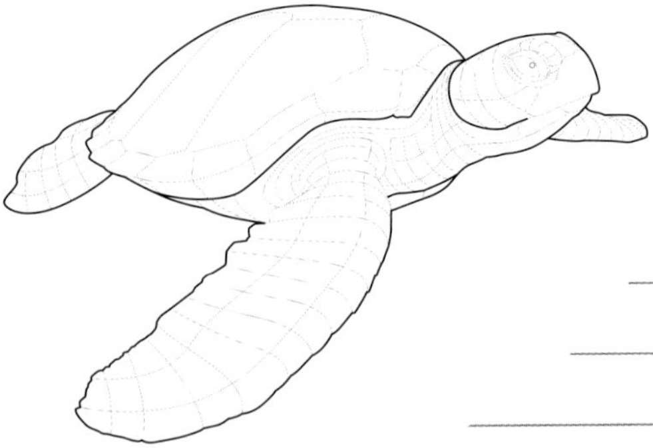

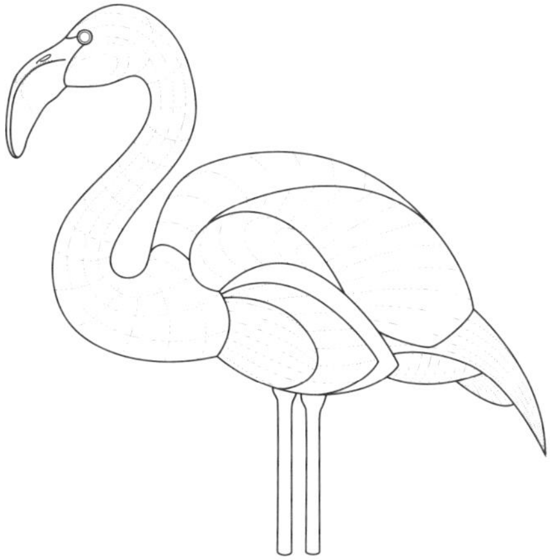

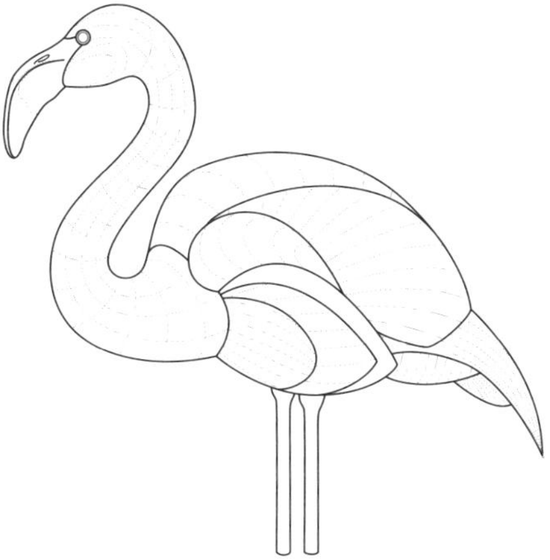

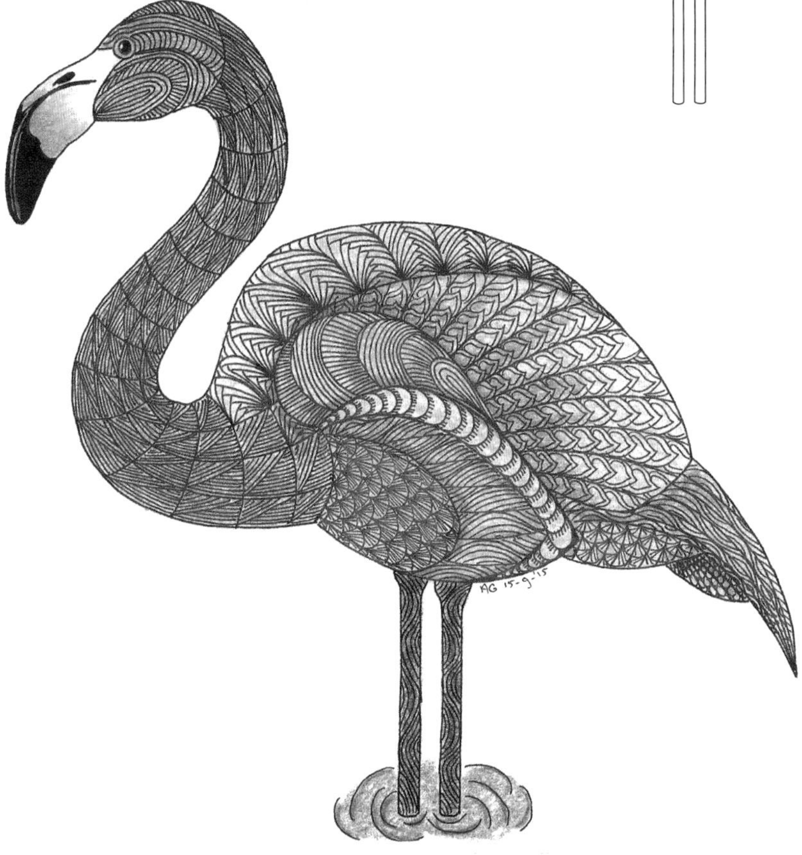
AG 15-9-'15

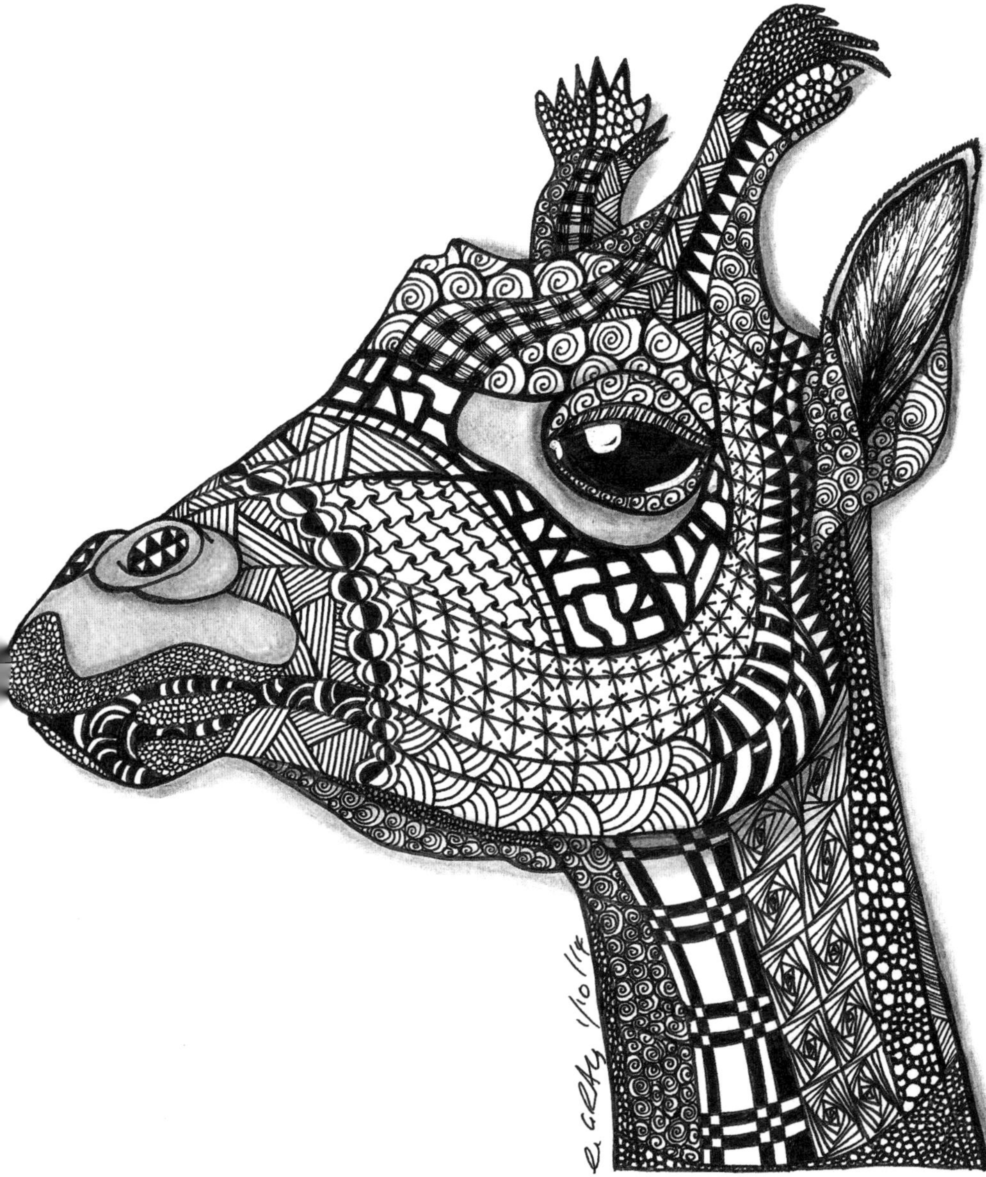

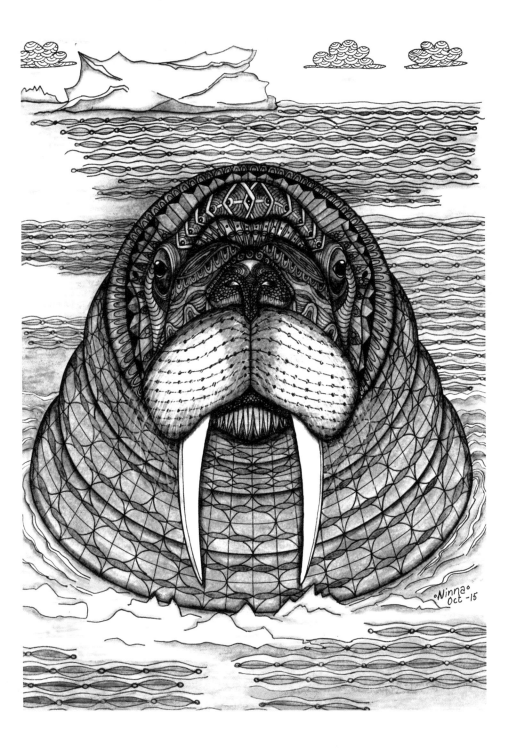
Ninna
Oct -15

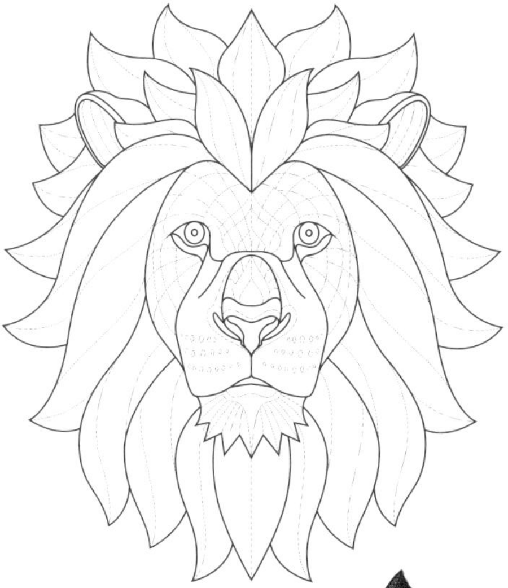
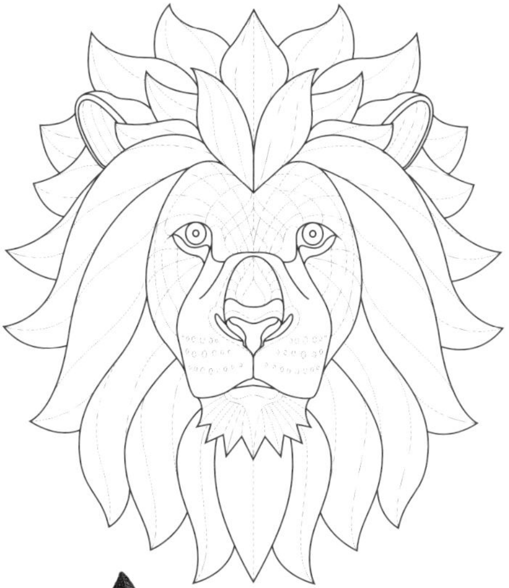
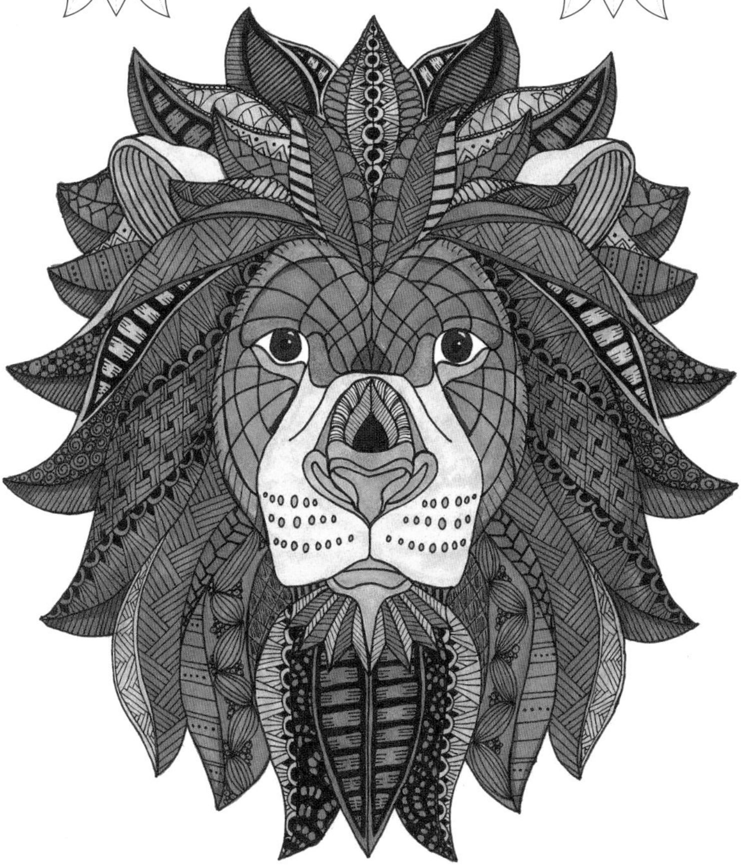

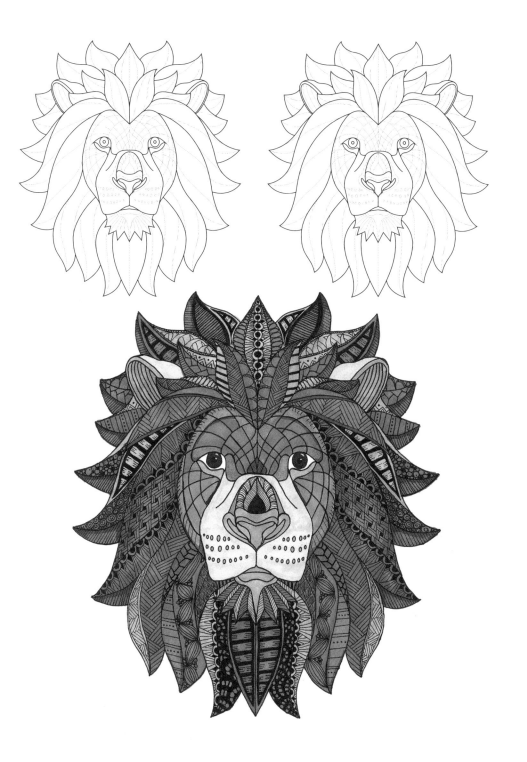

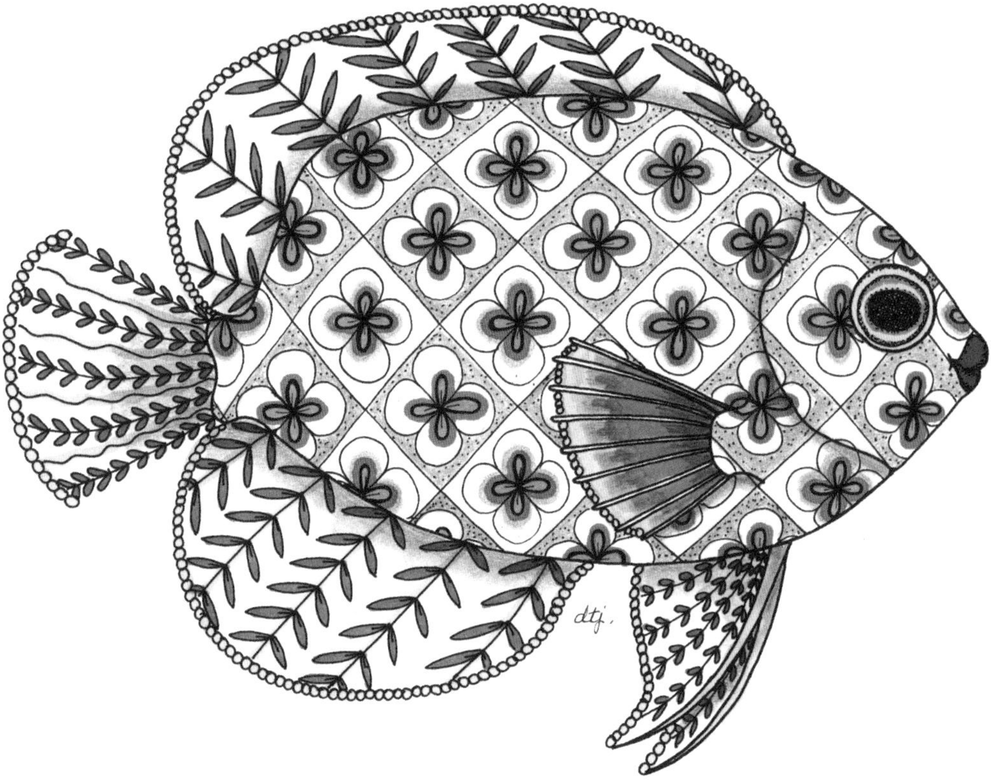
dtj.

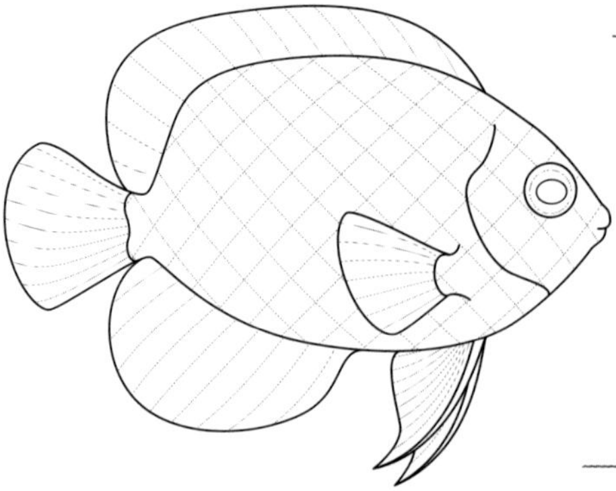

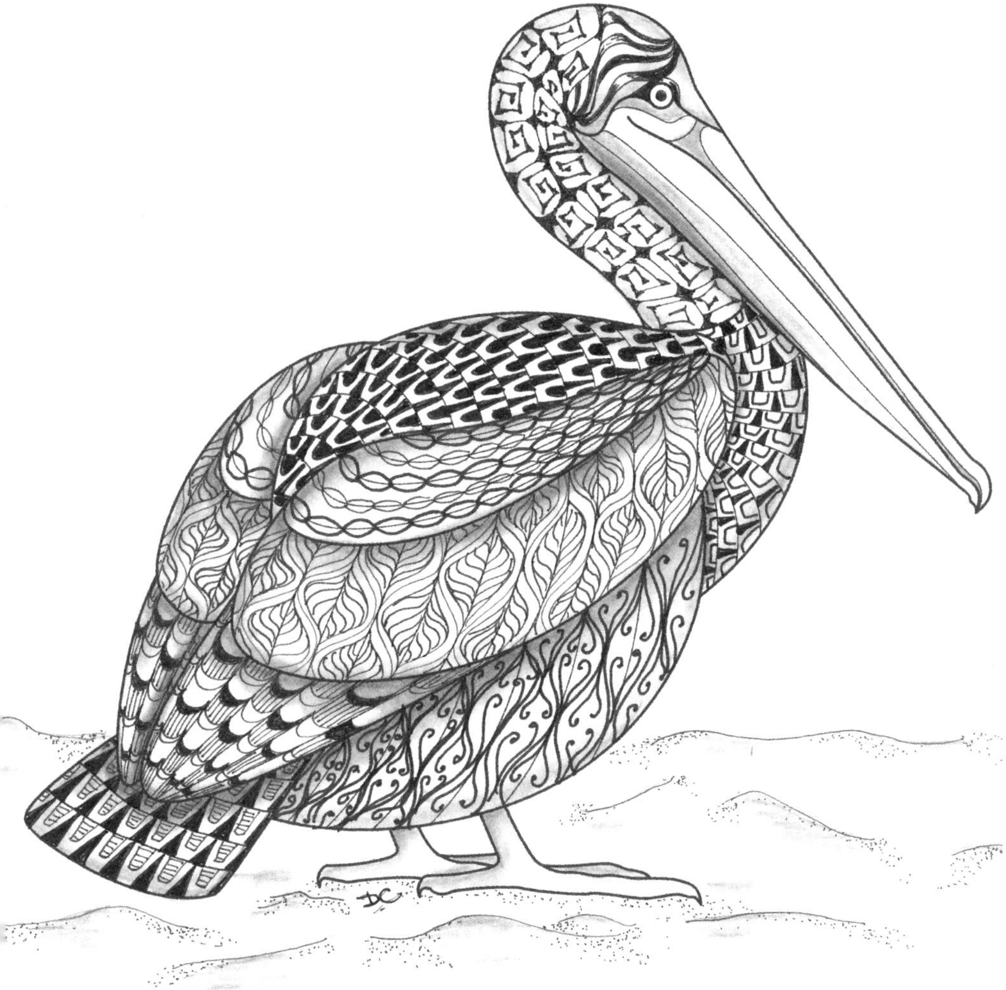
DC

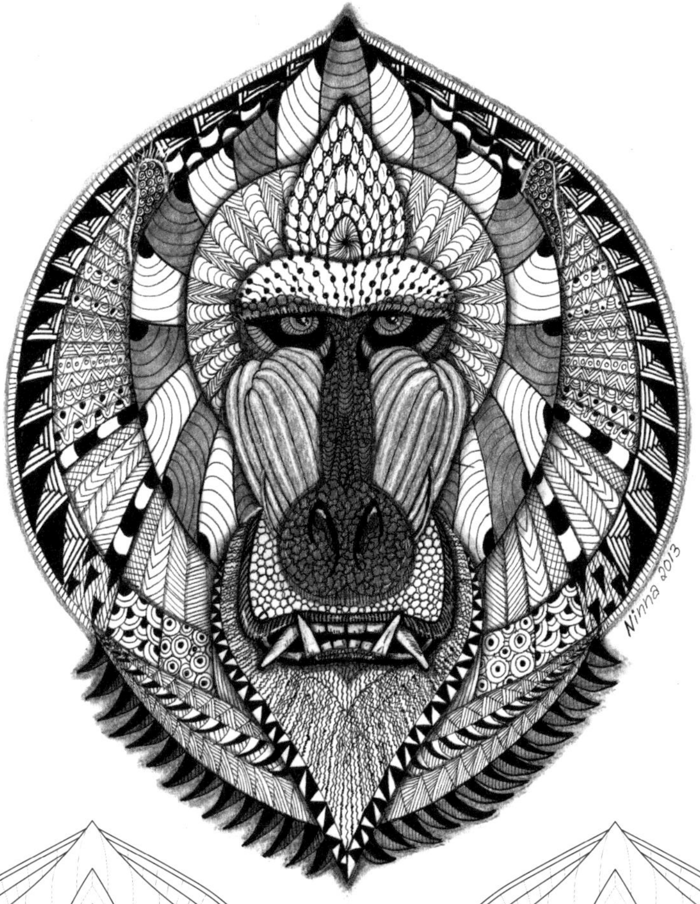
Ninna 2013

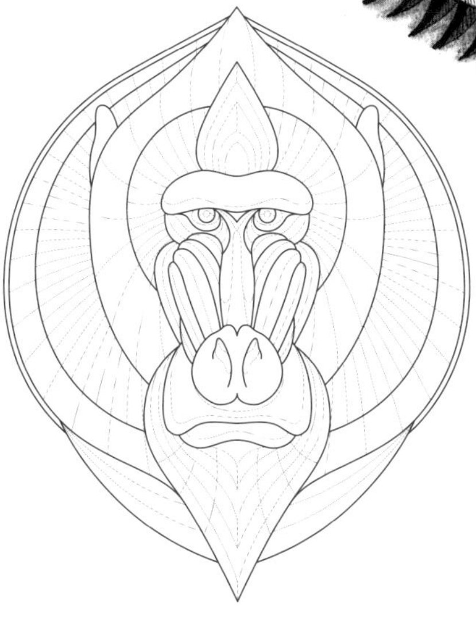

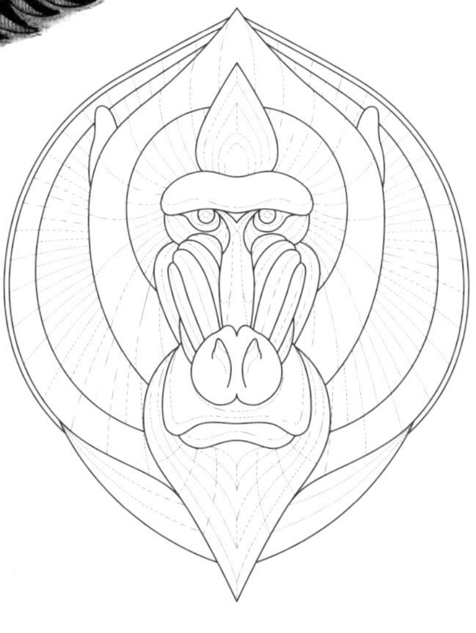

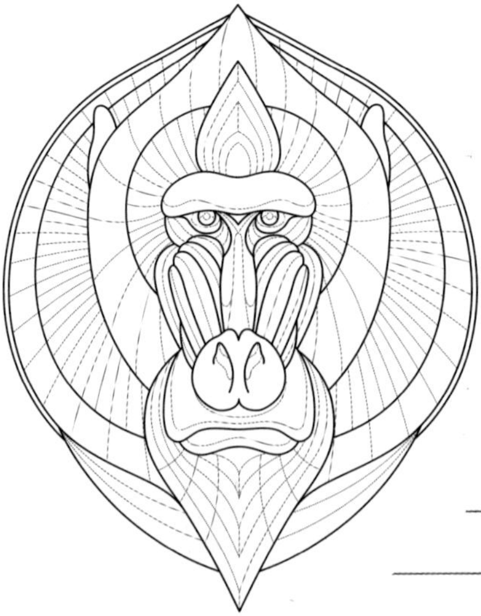

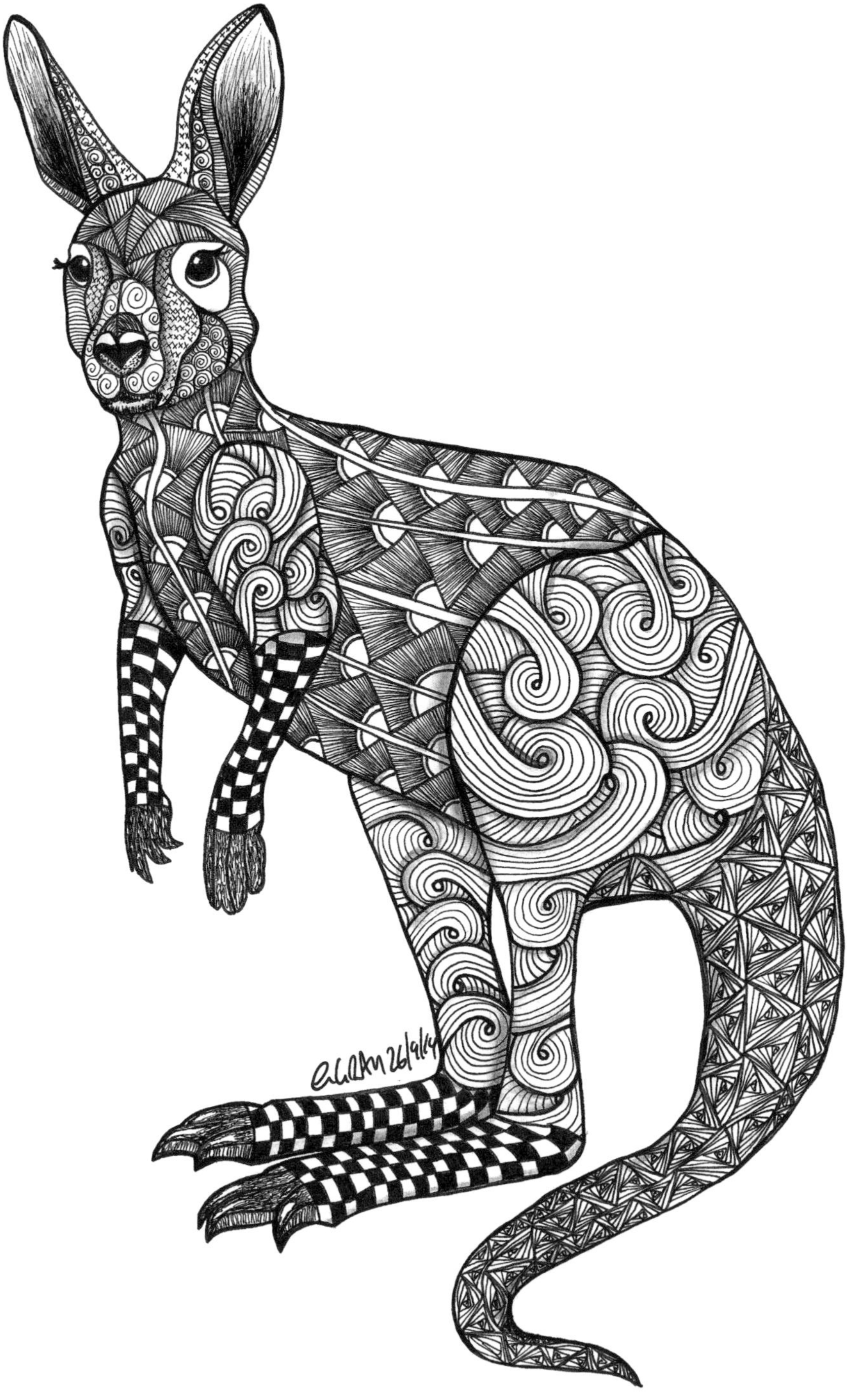
26/9/14

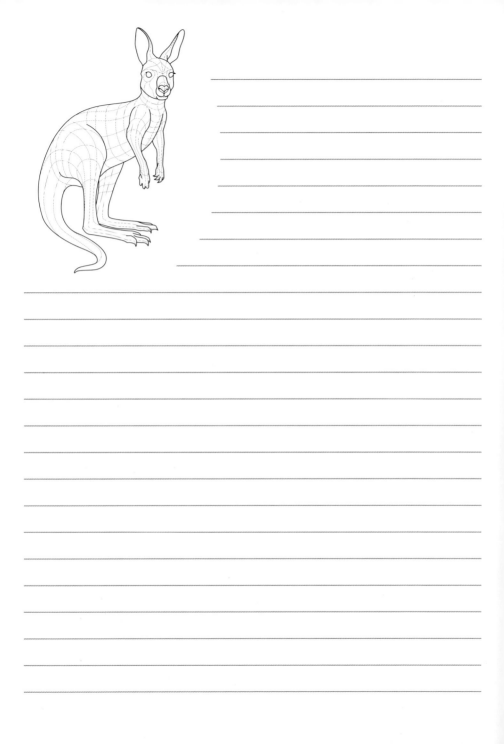

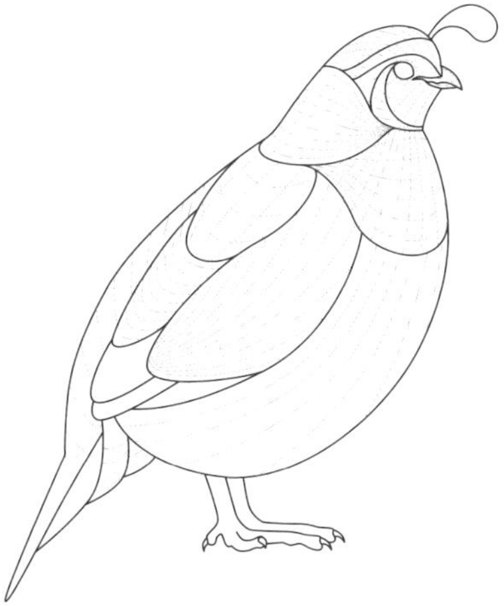

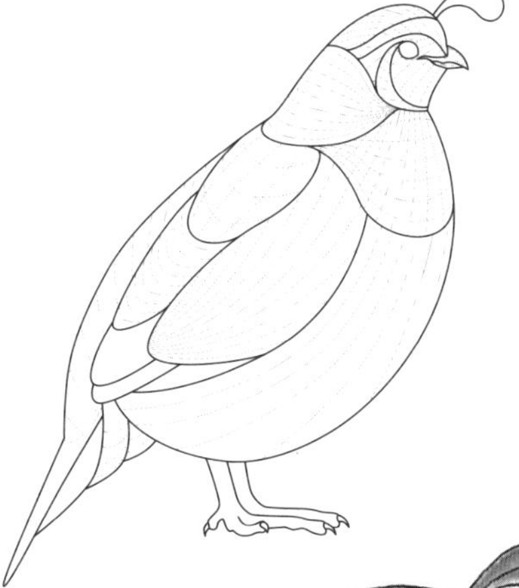

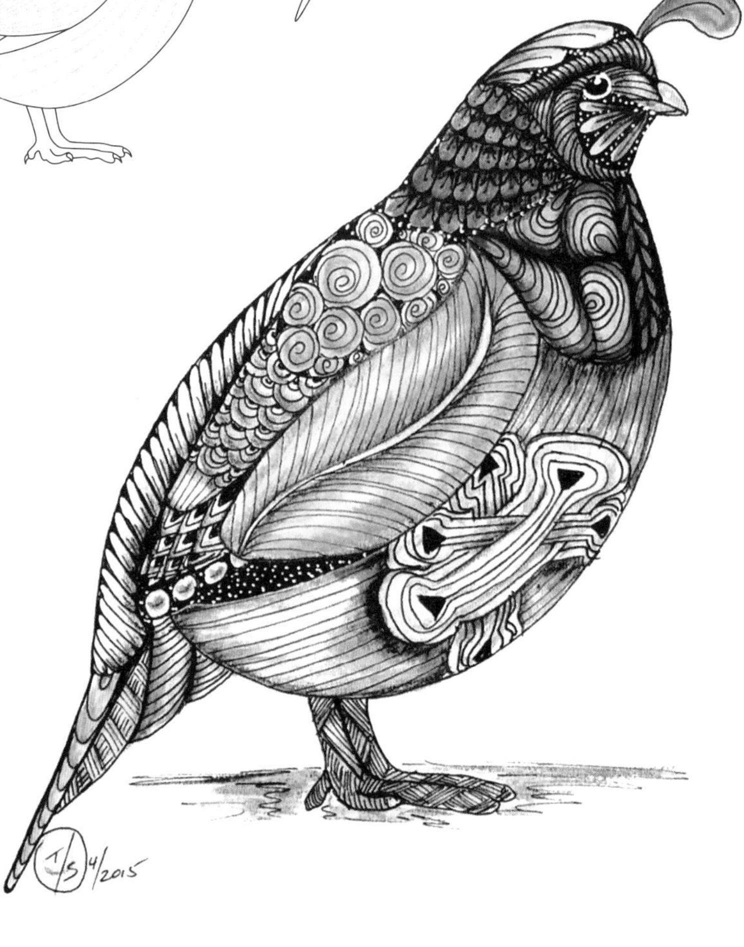
4/2015

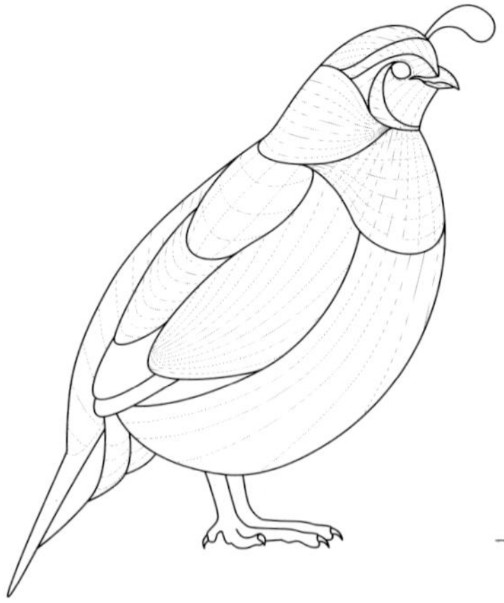

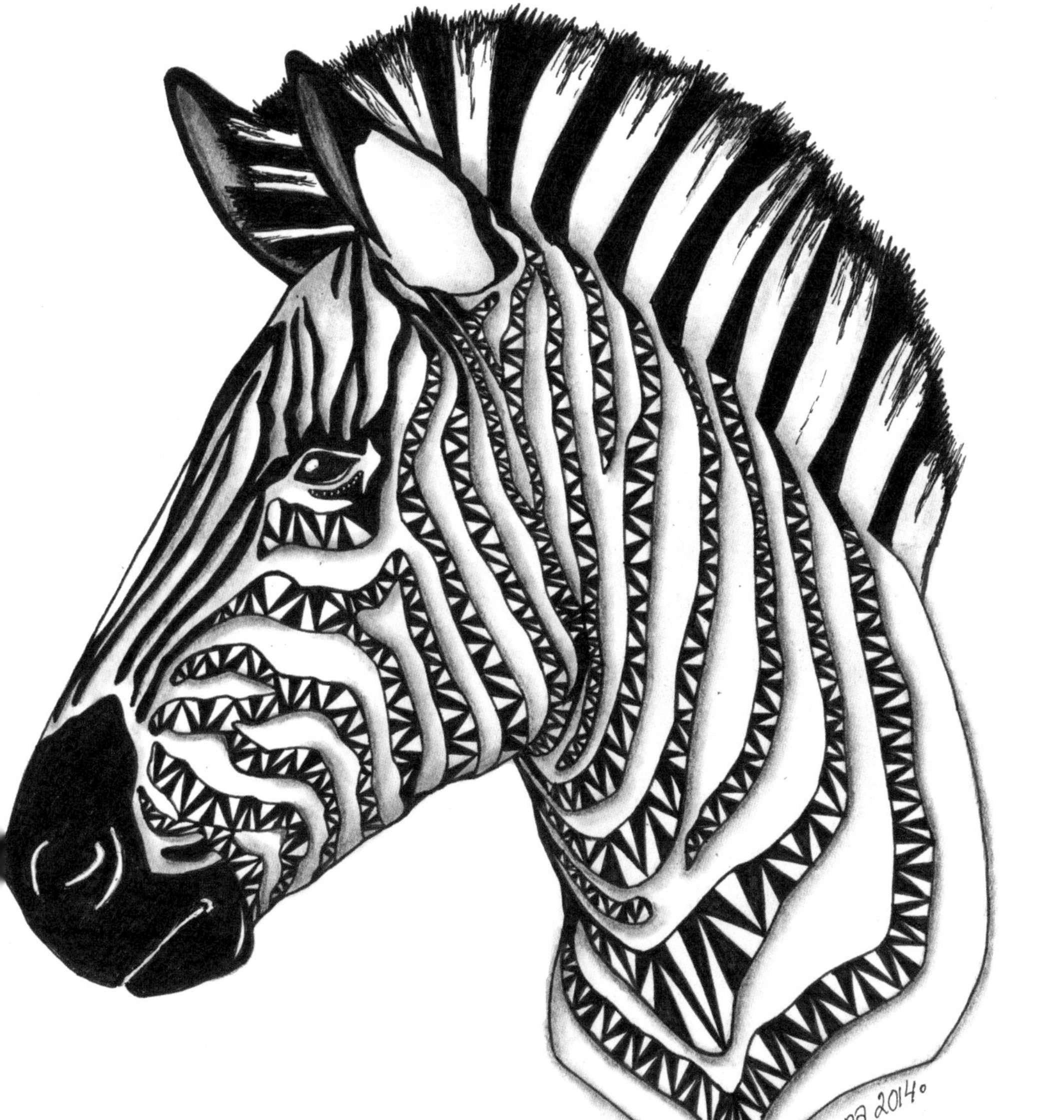
Ninna 2014

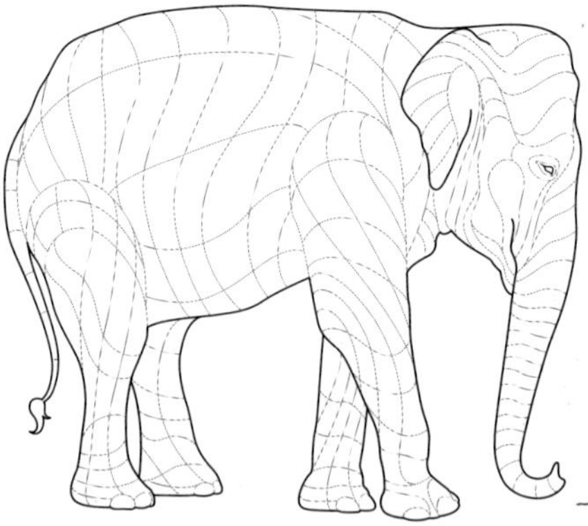

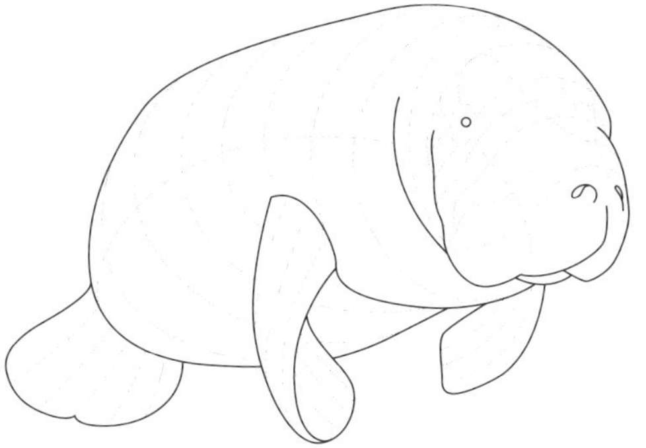

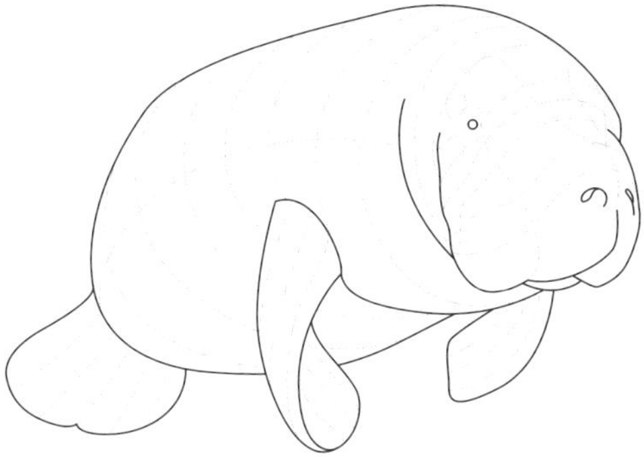

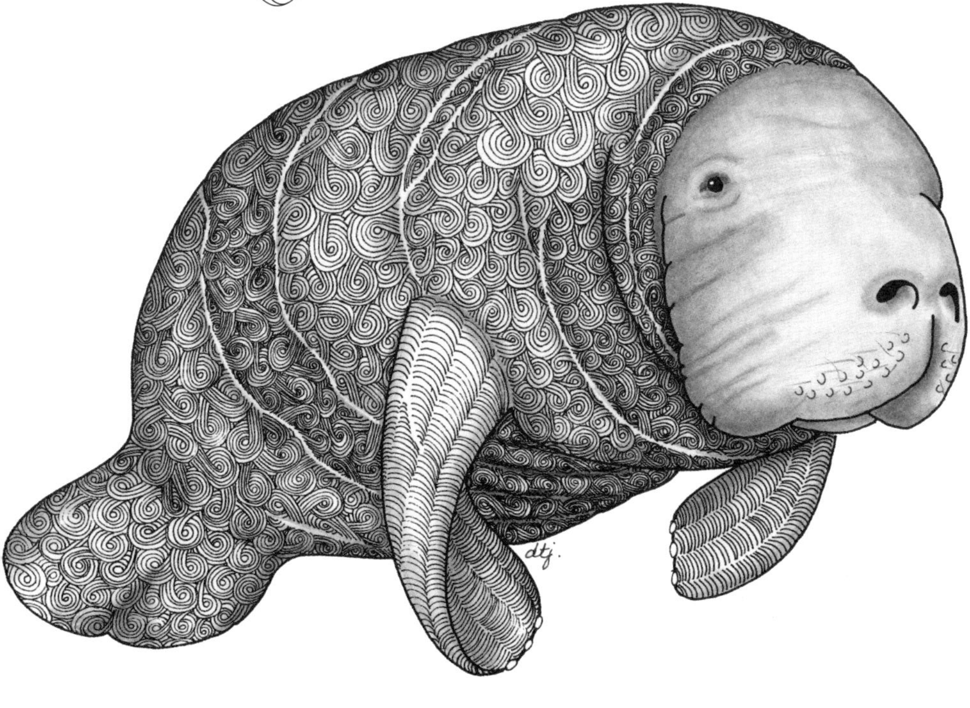
dtj.

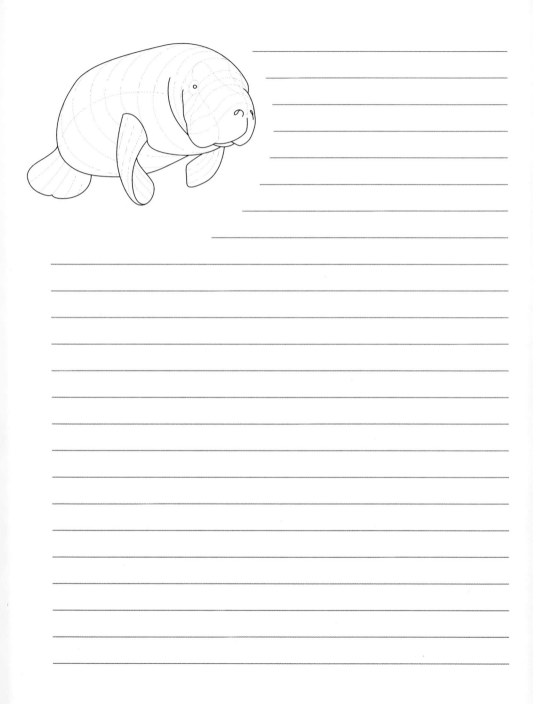

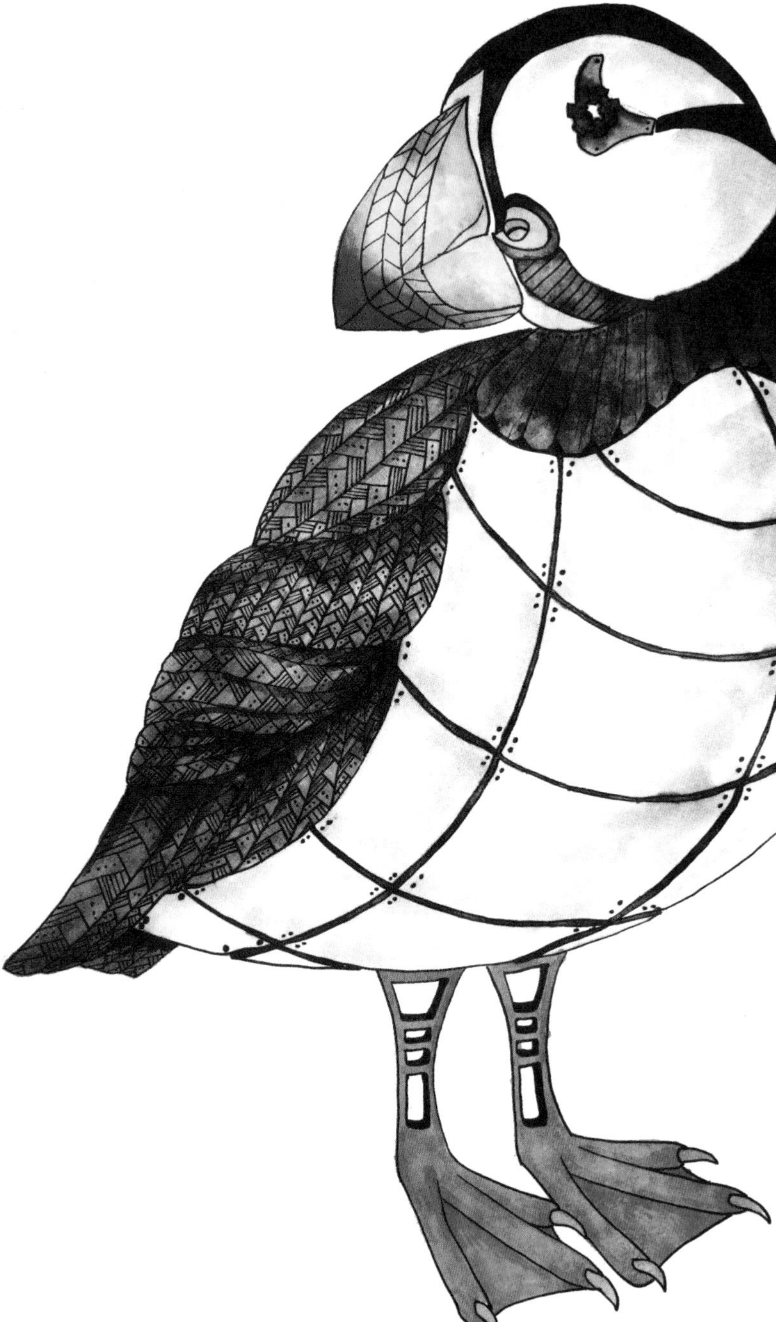

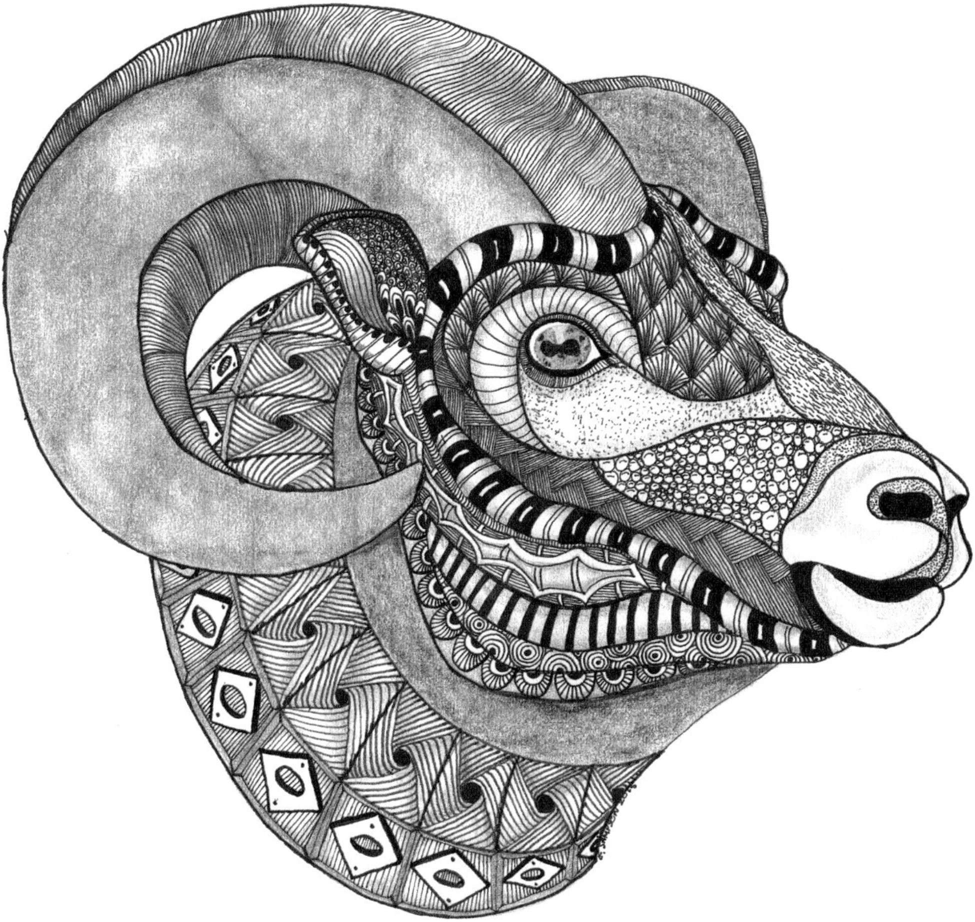

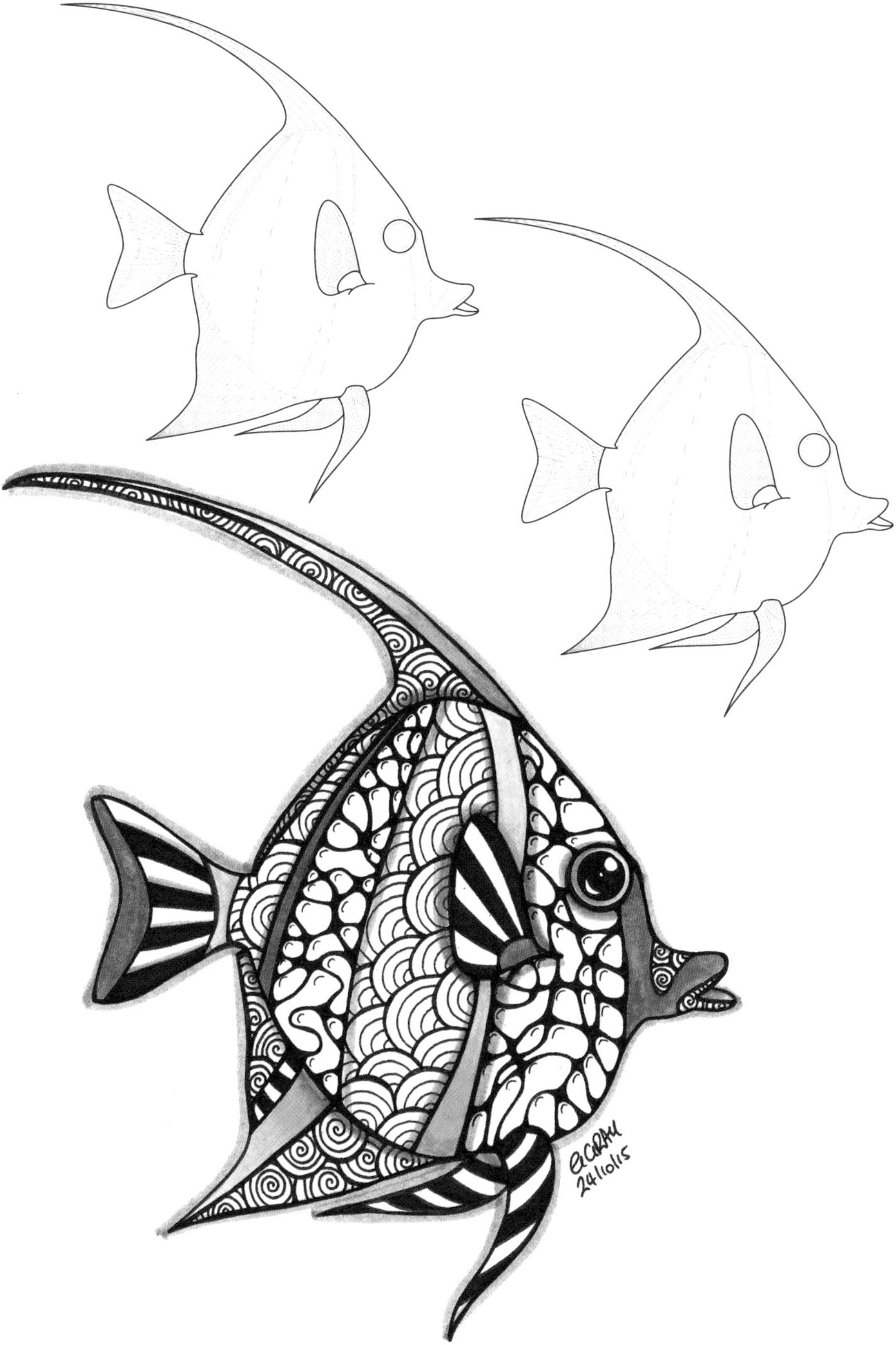
24/10/15

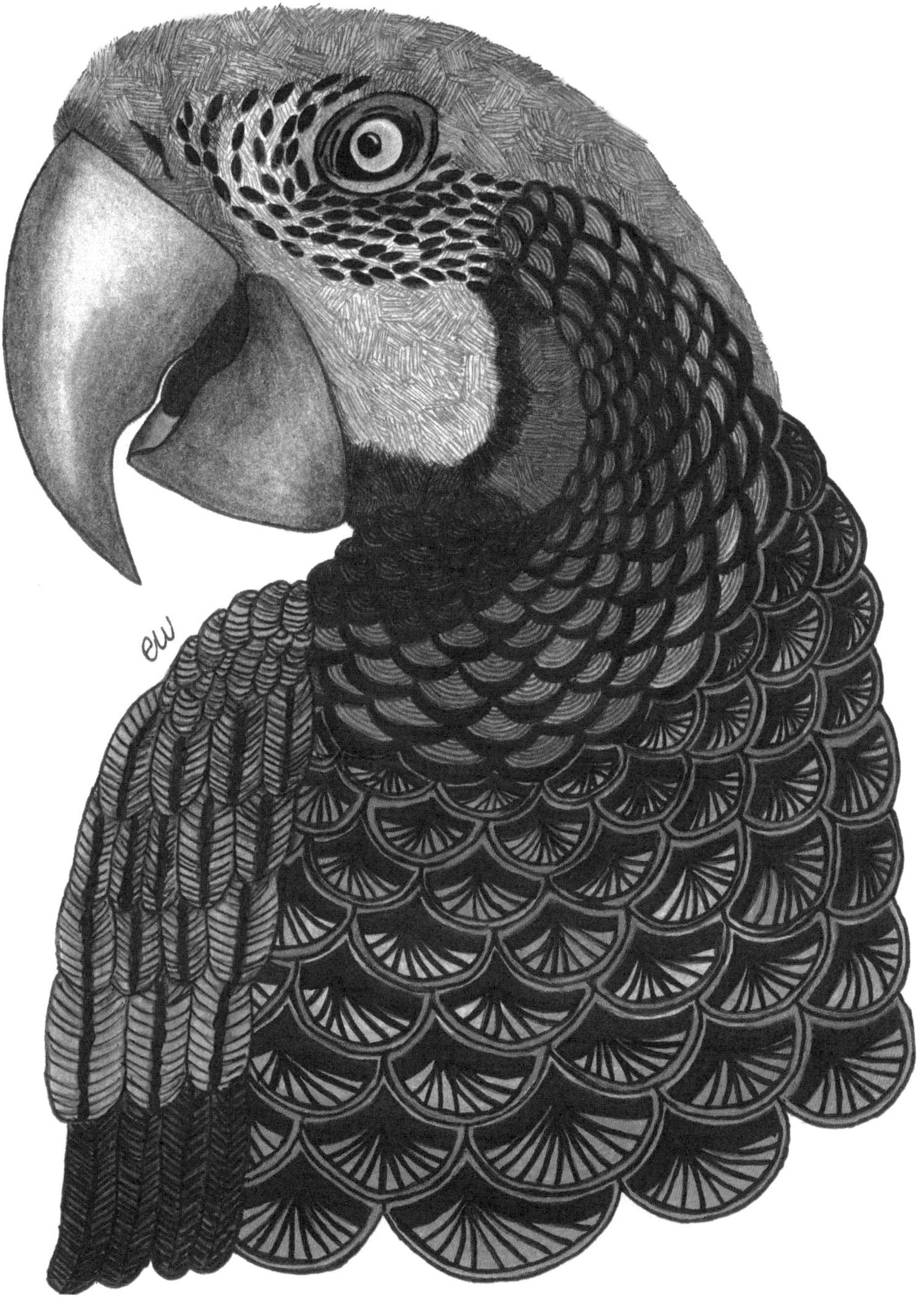

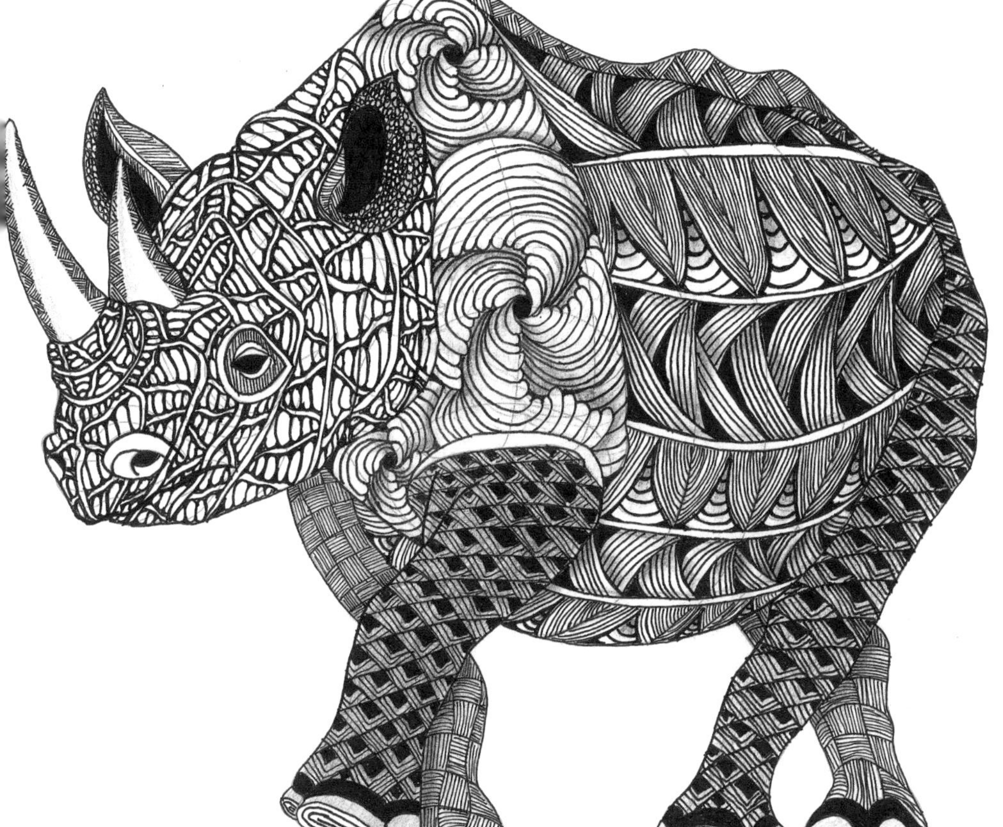

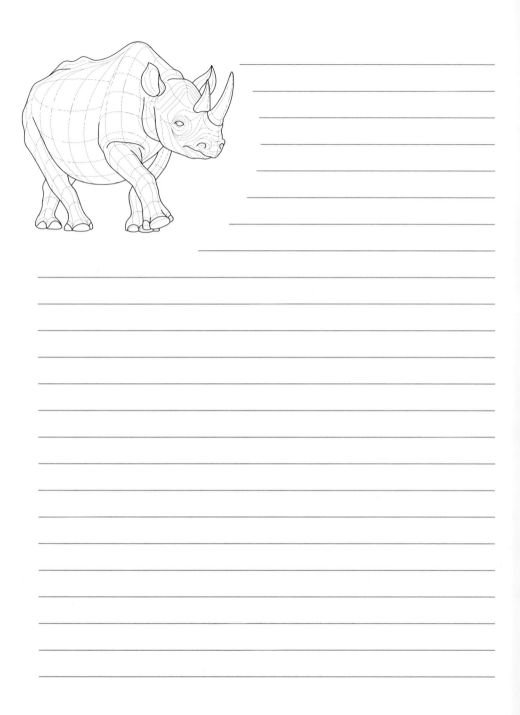

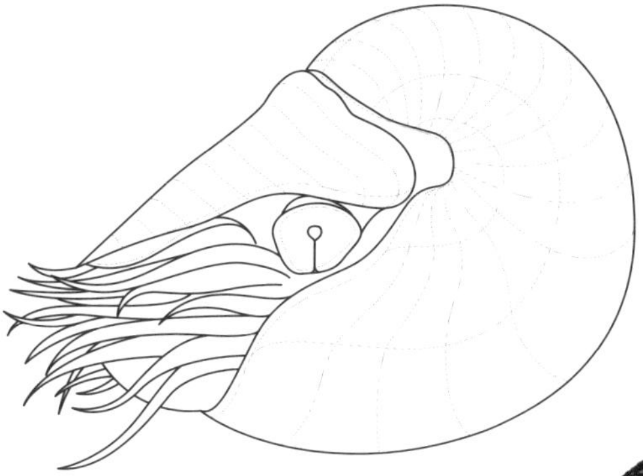

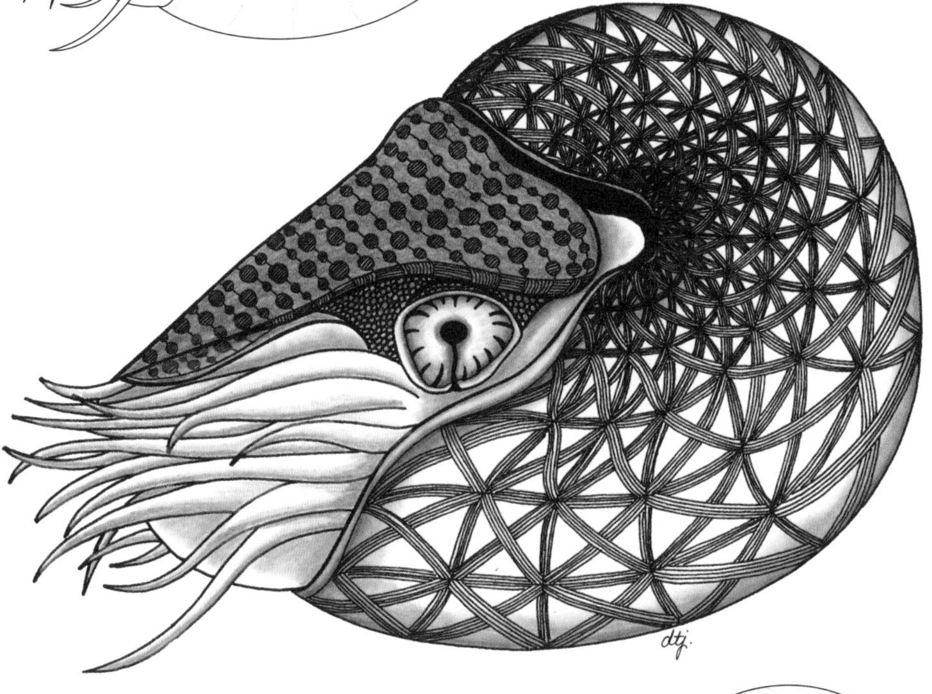
dtj.

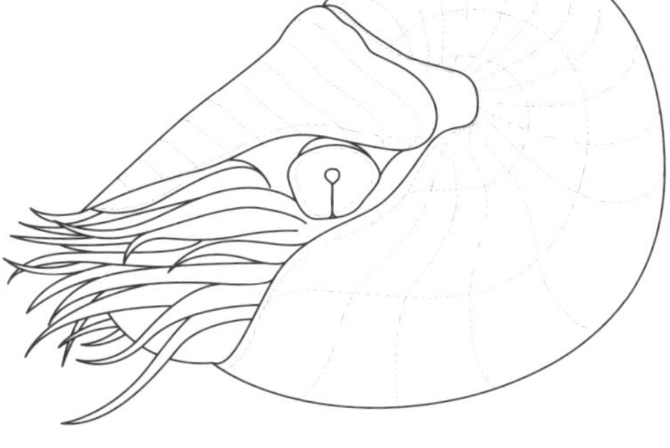

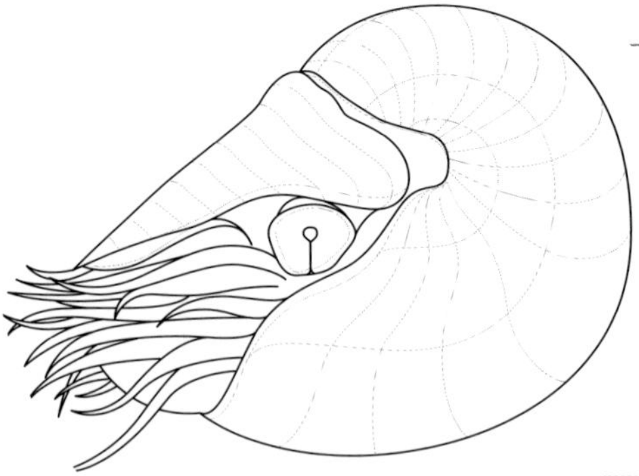

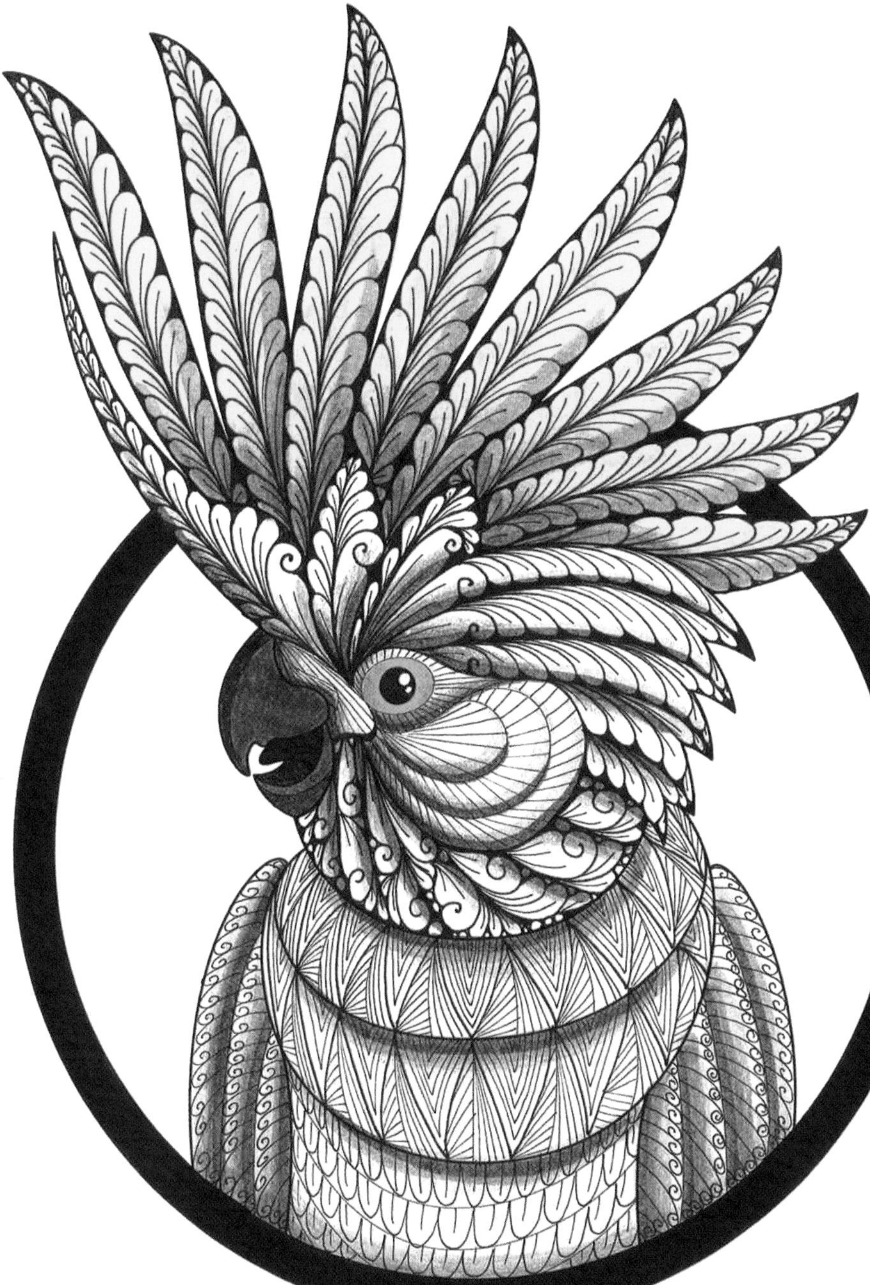

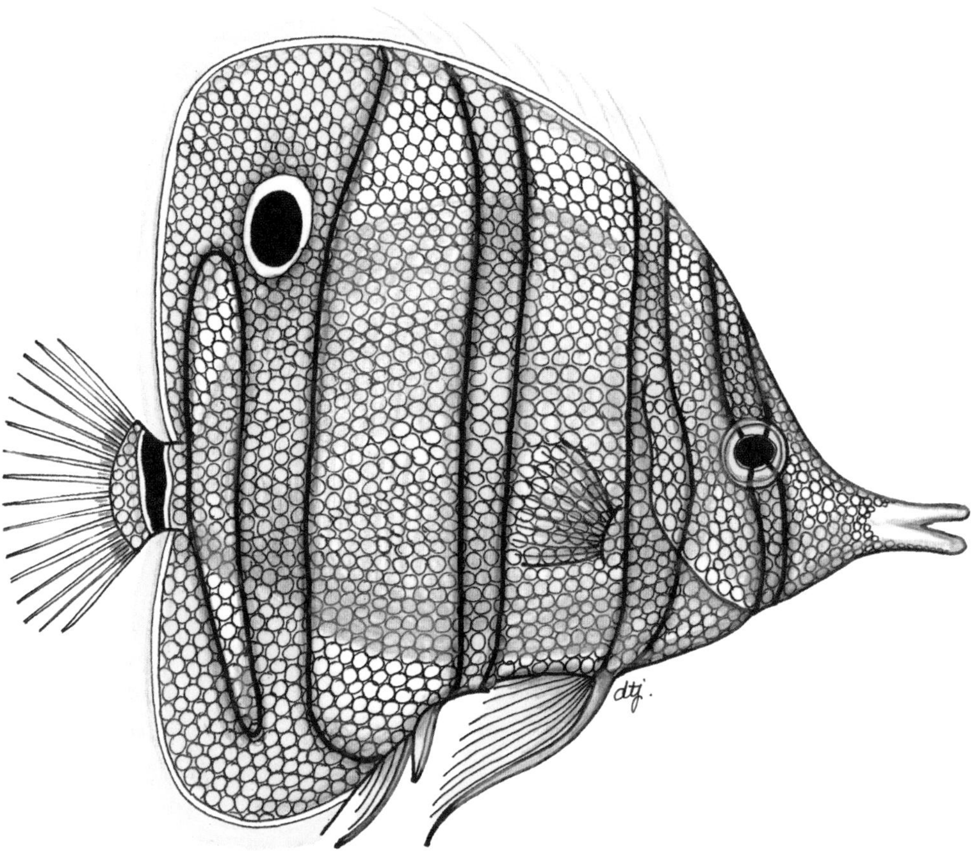
dtj.

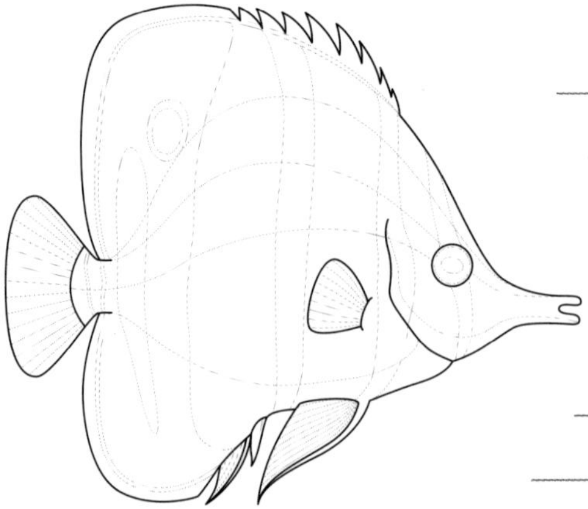

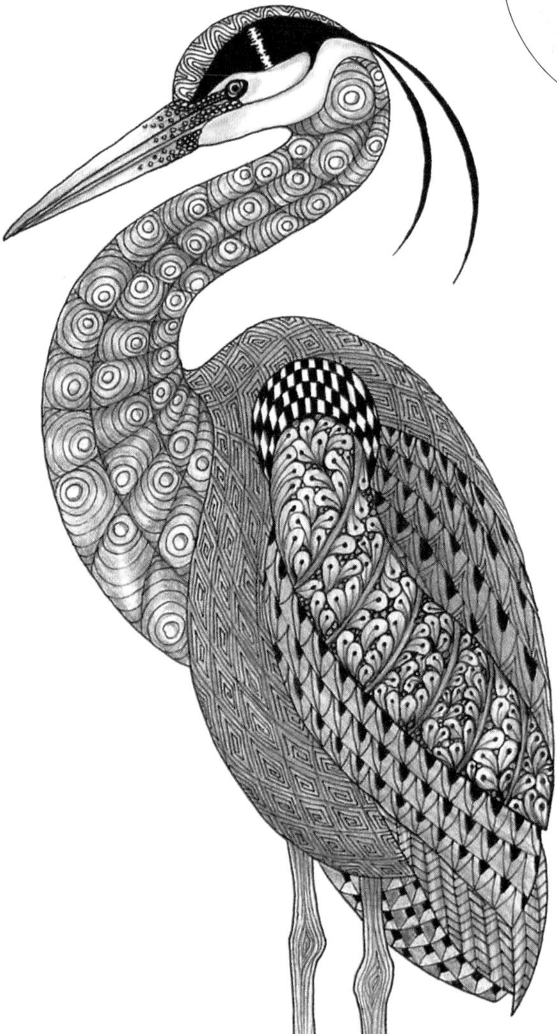

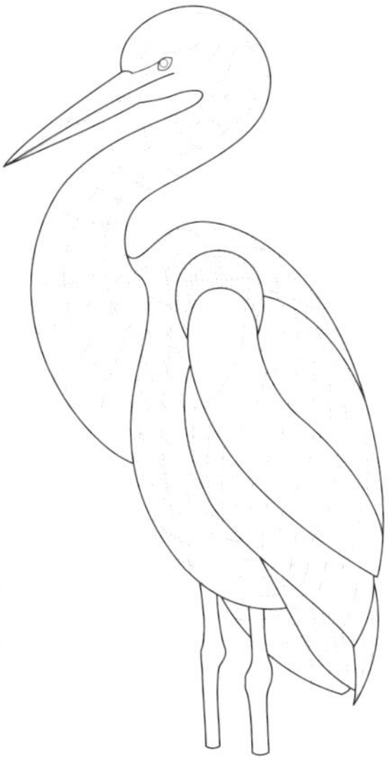

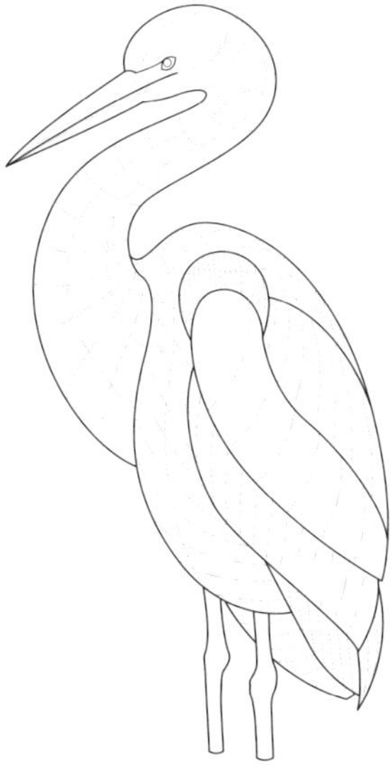

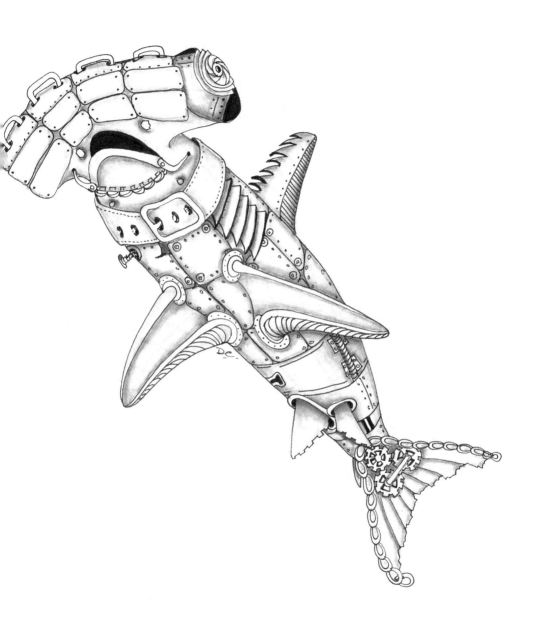

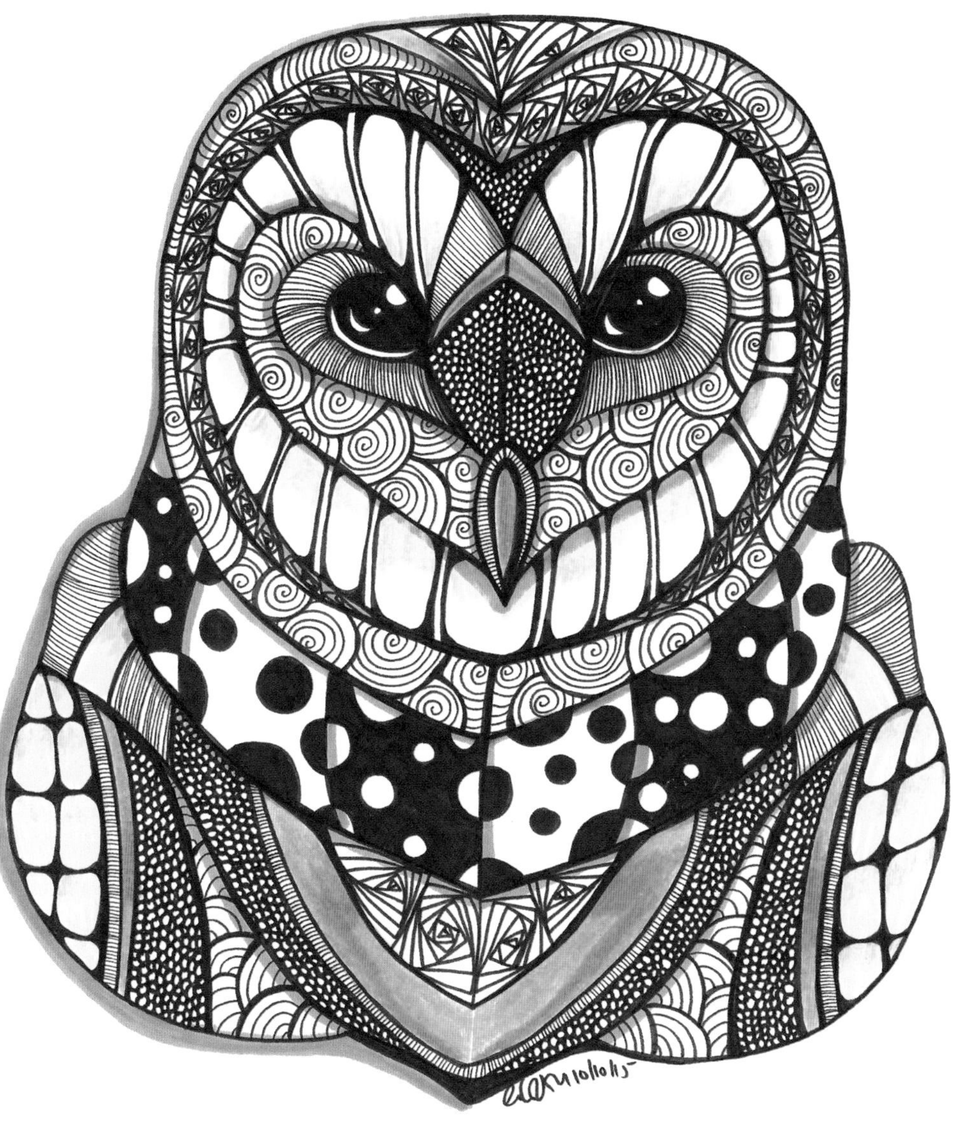

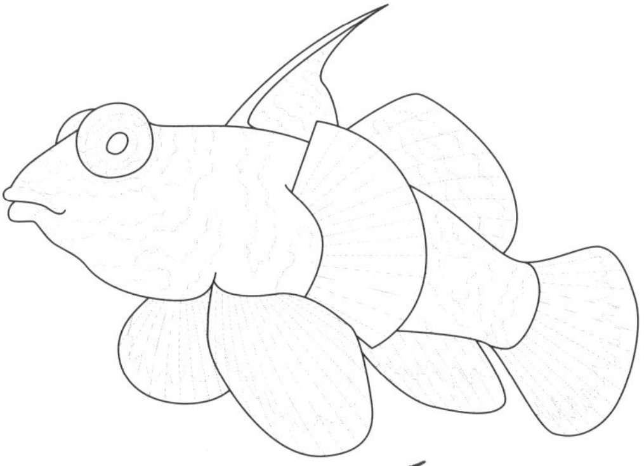

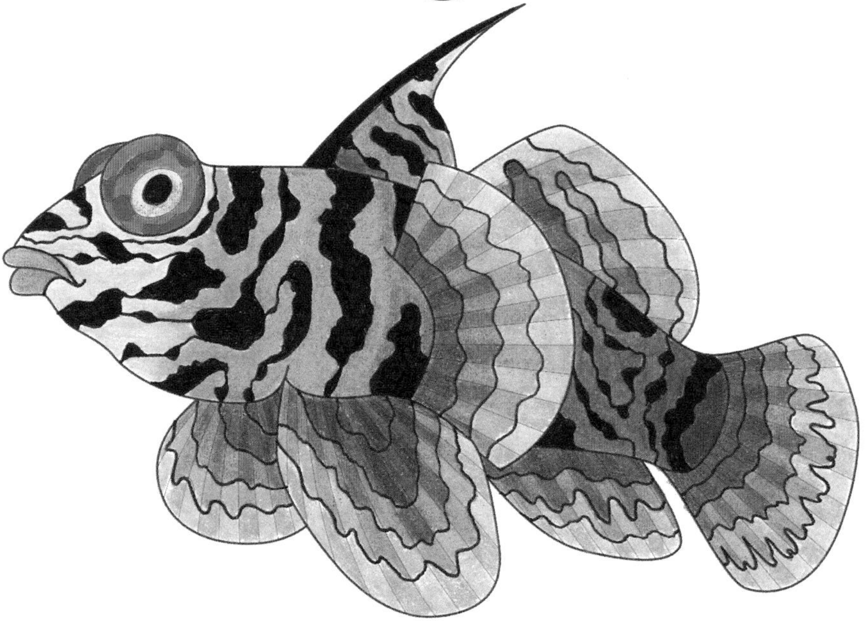

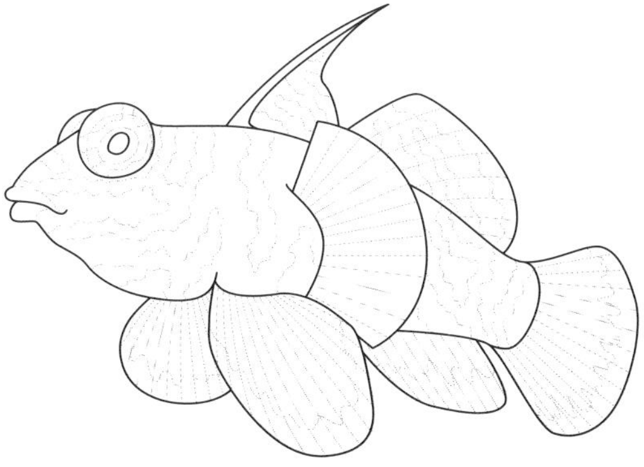

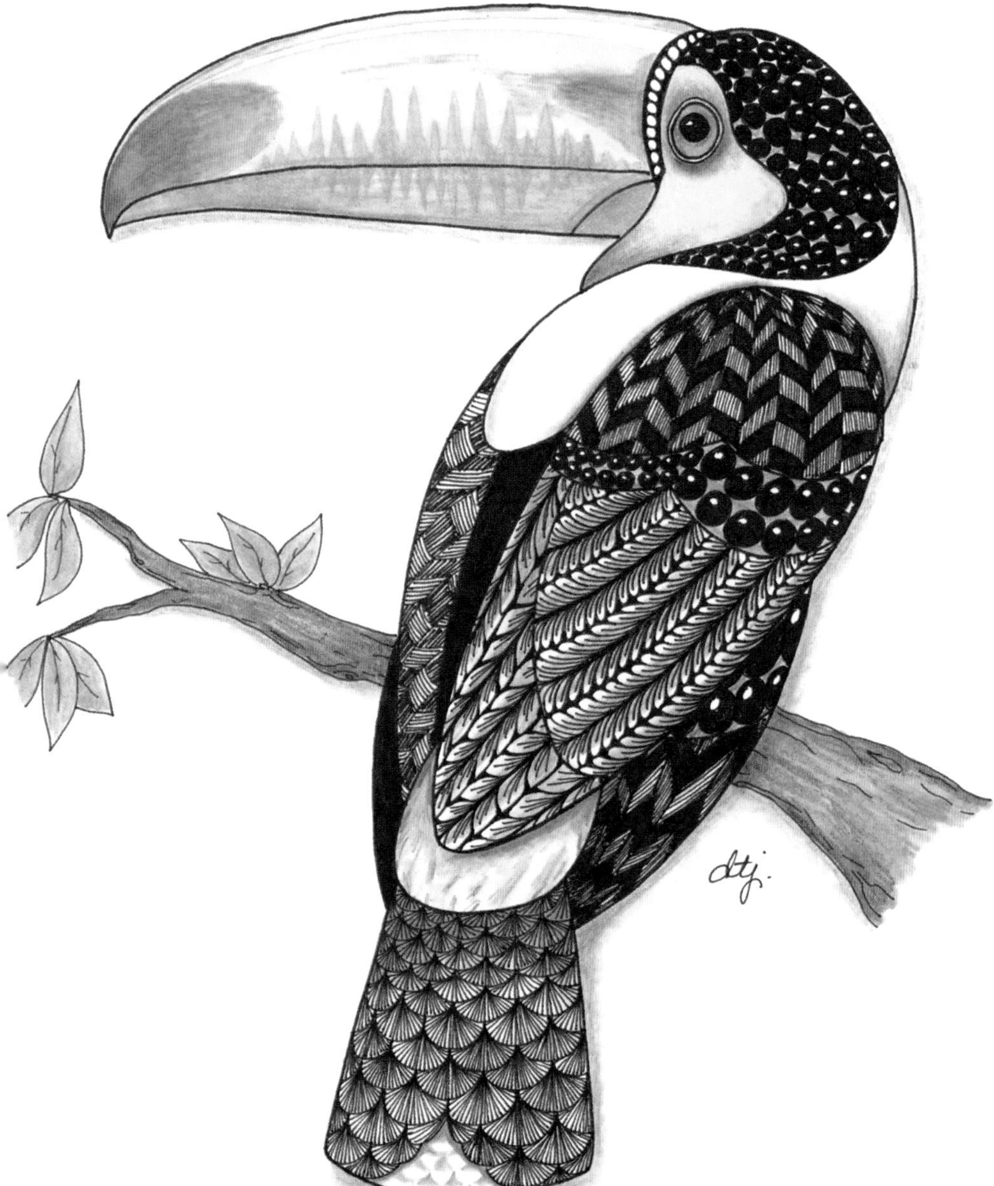
dtj.

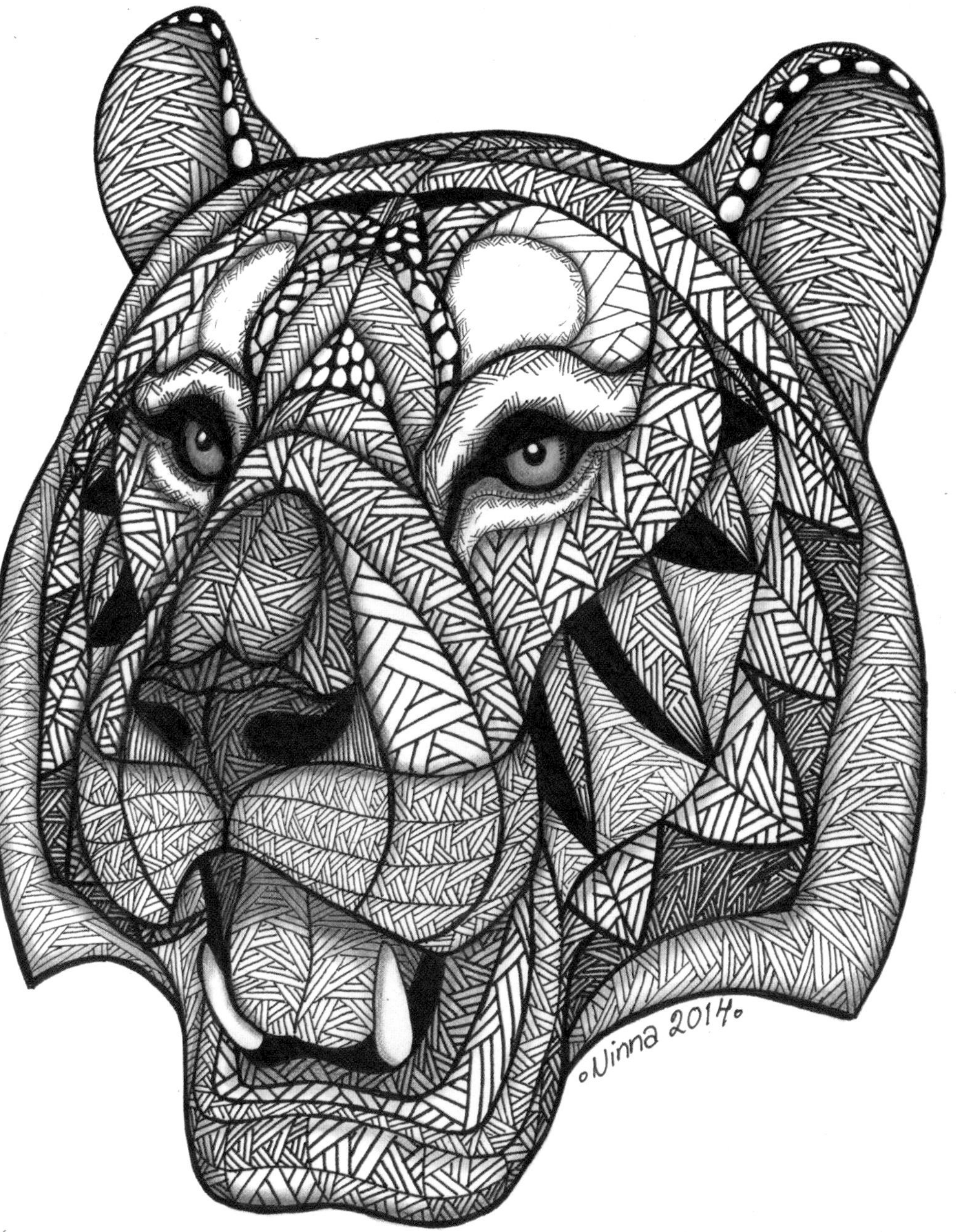
Ninna 2014

## About the Artist

Ben Kwok (a.k.a. BioWorkZ) is an L.A.-based professional graphic artist. Working as an apparel designer, BioWorkZ has developed his own highly original hand-drawn illustration style. His distinctive illustrations evoke the popular Zentangle® drawing method and his client list includes Red Bull, Converse and Lucky Brand. Ben encourages you to join him in supporting animal charities such as the World Wildlife Fund. *www.WorldWildlife.org*

## Other Craft & Drawing Titles from Ben Kwok

TangleEasy
Birds

TangleEasy
Lovable Pets
Design templates for Zentangle, coloring, and more

TangleEasy
Mandalas
Design templates for Zentangle, coloring, and more

TangleEasy
Meaningful Mandalas
and Sacred Symbols
Design templates for Zentangle, coloring, and more

TangleEasy
Wildlife Designs
Design templates for Zentangle, coloring, and more

---

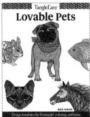

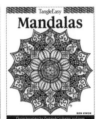

**Designs and Coloring by:**

Cover – Marie Browning, CZT

Ninna Hellman

Genevieve Crabe, CZT

Elaine Sampson

Adri van Gerderen

Abbey Gray

Erica Avedikian

Darla Tjelmeland

Dawn Collins

Karen Grayczk

Tina Sanders

Eva Wilson

Melissa Younger

---

ISBN 978-1-64178-010-0

Fox Chapel Publishing makes every effort to use environmentally friendly paper for printing.



We are always looking for talented authors. To submit an idea, please send a brief inquiry to acquisitions@foxchapelpublishing.com.

Printed in China
First printing

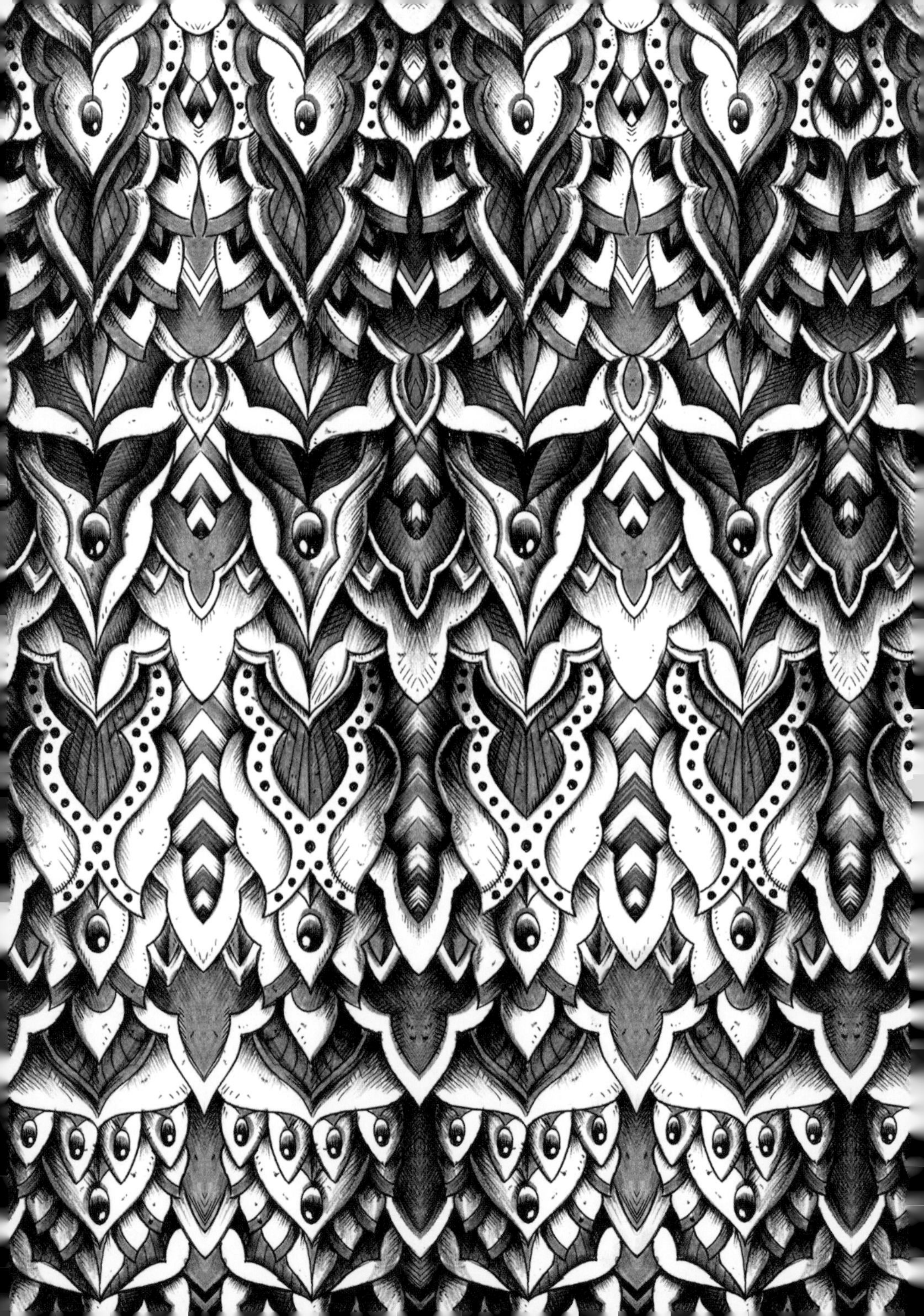